The Golden Boat

RABINDRANATH TAGORE

The Golden Boat

SELECTED POEMS

TRANSLATED AND INTRODUCED BY

JOE WINTER

ANVIL PRESS POETRY

Published in 2008
by Anvil Press Poetry Ltd
Neptune House   70 Royal Hill   London SE10 8RF
www.anvilpresspoetry.com

This book is published
with financial assistance from
Arts Council England

Set in Monotype Fournier by Anvil
Printed and bound in England
by Cromwell Press, Trowbridge, Wiltshire

ISBN 978 0 85646 406 5

A catalogue record for this book
is available from the British Library

to Rachana

I thank Susmita Bhattacharya and Devadatta Joardar for their unstinting help.

J. W.

Contents

Introduction

TO MEET A POET is to meet a mind. Rabindranath Tagore saw himself – knew himself – as a poet, though he was much besides: a prose-writer, painter, social activist and reformer; a patriot and an internationalist; a family man, a solitary; a public and private individual at once diffident in himself and charged with an expressive power. There was a necessary explicitness to his life that given its concerns was to leave a record of incalculable significance. One may turn to the prose, the plays, the short stories and novels, essays and lectures, to the paintings or to the letters or to the panoramic life itself, and learn much. The wild garden of the imagination, the practical vision, the edge to the intellect, the warmth of the man, can lead one to see with his eyes. Or one may explore in another way.

To stay at the centre, to turn more variously and more familiarly to the poems, is to travel no less far. At the notional point when all else is gone and only the art remains, the artist is finally present. Tagore was artist and practical man, the most visionary and the most level-headed of his time, it could be; to see the broad picture one must go outside the poems. But the depth of him is there.

In the double approach that many will take (if translation is to hand), a figure is to be glimpsed on the horizon that one can not cease to know. It is my view that Tagore had something to say for his time that is also to be said for the whole of human time. In this respect the poems are the underground support; the visible structure is in what he said and did elsewhere. But let the poems be enjoyed as poems, a half-century of his own moments of journey and arrival. Amartya Sen has written of their "astonishing beauty". If a touch of that remains I shall not have misled readers too far from the original. It came in many forms, each piece apart, all drawing together as one.

*

TAGORE was born in Calcutta in 1861 and died there in 1941. His life and work are well captured in Krishna Kripalani's *Rabindranath Tagore: a Biography* (OUP, London and the Grove Press, New York, 1962). The account breathes the man. Here I shall merely give a brief indication of the poetic corpus. Rather more than a quarter of his two hundred books were volumes of poetry, many with over a hundred pieces. As will be seen from the selection within, the poet often wrote at length, sometimes in lyric and sometimes in narrative verse. To many of his shorter poems he gave a melody and a re-born text to shape a song; while a host of other songs continually seemed to come from nowhere, musical impulses instinct with lightness, with sorrow, with yearning, with love: so that now there is a separate branch of Indian music formed entirely of his more than two thousand songs. They contain some of his purest poetry. He was primarily a lyricist and yet at the age of seventy was able to turn to prose-poems with a sudden leap into the here-and-now of an unvarnished reality. He continued to write in rhyme when the mood took him; and finally dictated from his death-bed a few terse poetic statements of a telling power. From his teens to his last days he was a prolific writer, uncannily gifted, and from first to last his poetic art was used in a spirit of *lila*. The term has in it the to-and-fro of a game of life, the individual as a playmate of the gods or destiny, the springs of laughter and compassion at once lying in a free acceptance of the state of play. "The Golden Boat", a famous early poem, that seems to carry a hint of a mystery at the heart of the self, is one of a number in which the unknown rules may be said to take over the game. It is with a slight sense of trespass, and more of risk and a certain recklessness, that I borrow the title for this collection.

*

WHO IS Tagore? I am not sure that either the East or the West (where for a time he was celebrated) has known the poet in the round. In West Bengal and Bangladesh, where Bengali is spoken and his poetry is cherished, the haunting melodious presence of so many of his songs has lent an air to the body of the poems, so that the more forceful of them often are neglected, or a melodrama is added to the recitation. A song is easeful in the way a spoken poem is not: so that a hint of luxury has come to clothe the idea of the poet, a soft glove on the hand that drove the pen. In the West, with his several volumes of self-translation into a limpid English prose, he drew on the glove himself.

It is of course the true poet who is appreciated in the original. It is simply like veering away from that aspect of a person that leaves one a touch uncomfortable. The raw encounter with the violence of life is everywhere in Tagore. A monsoon bombardment must be felt if the land is to be fruitful. If Bengalis of India and Bangladesh were not so much to deepen their acquaintance with their world-poet as to change it a little, the legacy could not be better invested.

The true poet was not appreciated in the West, even in the second decade of the last century at the time of the Nobel award for his English *Gitanjali*. A new prose-poet emerged, an exquisite English voice, the prayer of a pilgrim soul. It was a different beauty. Interest faded rapidly and after the poet's death fell away altogether. The first signs of a renewal of interest have been about for a little time and in their wake I offer these versions. I know the poet far less than those who have grown up with him, so to speak; but there may be an aspect to his verse that coming new to it I have caught. As to how to reflect it, an interesting question of poetics presents itself.

*

RHYME or not? A modern "voice" or not? Can a modern "voice" rhyme? Is to repeat the casing to dull the cadence? A host of queries revolves about a central one: can one transfer originality from the original? Or simply, is it possible to translate a poem?

Tagore had his doubts. Among a number of not entirely consistent statements of his on the topic was the view that a translated poem will lack the vitamins of the original. When he worked on a translation of a poem of his own he ended with something quite new. In its difference from its predecessor (often now in a decimated text, always altered in tone) it was if not a betrayal, at least an act of desertion. The old was left to drift like flotsam, so far as the new was concerned. It is the artist at work. There is still a state of confusion over the nature of the Tagorean "voice", as there has been so much translation from his translation, within India as well as without. In my view what is needed is to write poems that can delight as poems, that do not strike an attitude of one's own, and that singly and *in toto* carry the imprint of an all too elusive presence – the poetic personality of Tagore.

This of course changes from poem to poem; it is the poet at the time of writing that one has to catch. (And that Tagore did not.) I have kept the form, the casing, with an occasional minor change; and with it I hope a fresh cadence. Something of the original can be saved, re-created; what can not be is of the personality of the words themselves. I can not begin to capture the atmospherics of the Bengali language. To give an example of its richness: there is a phrase in "My Last Spring" ("Shesh Basanta") that it is virtually an insult to re-phrase. *Benubanachchhayaghana sandhyay* means "into the evening's darkening shade / of a thicket of bamboo" as I have given it. But the first word (my fourth to tenth) has a magical rustle and depth to it. The sleight of a Sanskrit-derived tongue for compound words and rhyme finds a moment of onomatopoeia that is not to be repeated except in the same syllables. Part of the personality of the poet is forever woven in the dark grove of his words. But I too have a language and something can be done with it. The poet is more than his local medium. Can a poem be translated? The answer is more yes than no. Can Tagore's force be conveyed by what to many now is an outdated artifice? If he wrote in rhyme, rhyme can be used; and while such effects are possible within the play of language, they can be used in the play of a poem. Poetry is the *lila* of every land and tongue.

*

WE TURN to the great daring of the poems themselves. Is not a poem the loneliest journey an individual can make? From this small selection the reader may sense something of the experience Rabindranath gained, and the direction he took, on the oceanic voyage. There could be a hundred other collections of a similar size with as many new poems as old in each. I include a number of the best-known pieces but by no means all. I do not have the time, the book does not have the room, nor may the reader have the room herself for more as she comes to glimpse the odyssey, to apprehend the expanse. I did not feel the poems needed a potted biography: it was the sort of thing the poet himself abhorred. "Where is the poet?" he asked when someone had researched and written the story of his life. The poet is in what comes next.

JOE WINTER
2006

Disenchantment

I know at last that my night's dream is gone.
The garland's flowers are dead, the string stays on.
  Now no more a stealing-of-glances,
    swift retreats and close advances –
now eyes merely see, without love's sign.
The tendril of your arm imprisons mine.

No smile now to tug at the lower lip.
No special secret not to be let slip.
  At your voice no overflowing,
    my heart about my body going . . .
nor at your song do my eyes fill with brine.
No need to brush away a tear's salt line.

Upon the Earth the Spring is no more fair,
the moonlit night of youth and life is bare.
  Are a *veena*'s strings soft-ringing?
  Who knows where the flowers are springing?
Who will come to pluck those flowers so fine,
to weave and weave them to a wreath's design?

A flute sang, I surrendered – it was dumb.
And now chains weigh me down and I am numb.
  Sweet nights are past: remembering
    brings on the heart's belabouring.
No joy but an illusory false shine.
No love – though we caress and sigh and pine.

How often have you lain there, in night's sighs,
and searched my wan face with your tender eyes!
    To bear another's grief must weaken –
    so your body wilts, grief-stricken –
as I lie still with hard heart and malign.
Sleep, sleep – to weary sleep your soul resign.

1887

Sea-Waves

on the sinking of a boat taking pilgrims to Puri

It swirls in Ruin's vast-hurling,
the shoreless sea upcurling,
    savagely festive;
flapping a hundred wings,
the wind with the pomp of kings
    swaggers high-restive;
knit stark-mad together
are sky and sea in each other,
    the world's-eye dark-veiling;
in lightning's quailing-and-quaking
inanimate Nature is shaking
    with harsh-quick-white laughs, a foam-wailing.
These demons, homeless, blind,
deaf, loveless, crazed in mind,
    tear loose from every tie
    and run to die.

To all shores it is lost,
the blue sea dark-tossed,
    its cries outpouring,
its fear, its rage gasping,
its laughter sheer-rasping,
    wildly roaring,
boiling, self-slivering,
to grains-of-dust shivering,
    for its lost shores all-about-crashing —
as if Vasuki, world-bearing,

his thousand hoods flaring,
     dropped his burden in sport, his tail lashing!
As if the liquid night,
pulled apart by its own might,
     had sundered its own net of sleep,
          to slip free in the deep.

It has no tune, no pulse,
to meaning, to joy it is false,
     the dance of the unalive.
Is it that great Death
from a thousand lives takes a breath,
     to dance, to thrive?
Water thunder vapour air,
blind-alive from somewhere,
     new-nerved, despairingly free,
without direction or way,
without stop, without stay,
     self-afraid, to Destruction they flee.
Within them see then
eight hundred women and men
     embracing, keeping Death out –
          even while gazing about.

The storm demoness claws
the boat round and roars
     Give, give, give!
Says the sea foam-showering,
with a million arms towering,
     Give, give, give!
Frustrated in hunger,

frothing, heaving in anger,
　　the blue death turns white in sheer fury.
The small ship is overborne,
its iron breast must be torn,
　　its cargo no more may it carry.
Up and Down flip a plaything
as if it were nothing.
　　Still in the boat's prow
　　　　stands the helmsman now.

Men and women cry out there
God, God, hear our prayer,
　　your mercy give!
Again and again the pitiful cries,
again and again their voices rise,
　　Let us live!
Those oldest friends of ours,
sun and moon, where? Where the stars?
　　Where Earth's lap that we shared together?
Where home and hearth,
our first love from birth –
　　how wild this demoness stepmother!
Round us nothing's known,
nothing's here of our own –
　　awful faces of strange form
　　　　everywhere swarm.

The flooring is split,
a torrent drives up from it,
　　the ocean's jaws gape, unforgiving.
God, you are none,

kindness, life, you are gone –
   we are morsels for the unliving.
Frightened by fear
children scream. Life is here,
    life is gone. In an eye-blink it's finished.
That awful lament,
who can say when it went,
    when an outcry all at once vanished?
As if the same gale
made a hundred lamps fail –
   in a thousand homes all about
     it descends. Joy is out.

Others' hurt, its own,
to it is unknown,
   this lifeless madness.
Why is the human mind
trapped there, confined
   in pain, in love's gladness?
Brother embraces brother,
a child looks to its mother.
    What is a mother's love for girl and boy?
In the sun's sweet rays
a love-game still plays
    so long of such grief and such joy!
In hope's trembling dream
why should a tear gleam?
   A merest lamp's flame quivering,
    love's fearful shivering.

How bravely the race
is rocked in its place
   in a lifeless lap!
Why is hope's breath
by the monster of death
   not swallowed up?
With her last ebb of life
to hold her child safe
   a mother leaps forth.
She will not give it up,
even running deep
   into death's mouth!
There on the one hand
ocean and sky stand,
   she on the other –
      who takes them, the infant and mother?

From where this great might
to clasp her child tight
   even then, even there?
In this unliving numb
cruel stream – love has come
   to the heart from where?
Despair is not hers,
she accepts no reverse –
   but an ever-sweet nectar, no other.
If such a heart
has the tiniest part
   in a world, then a world has a mother.

In a world-wide ruin
it seems, a slight woman
   puts death to flight, for love's sake.
      What Woman has kept Love awake?

To one place, side by side,
terribly allied,
   kindness, unkindness have come.
Great hope, great fear
make a dwelling here,
   together sharing a home.
To know false from true
pierces us through –
   the heart travels far, travels near.
The Unliving One fells,
all prayers he repels –
   Love welcomes, dispelling all fear.
Are there two gods
forever at odds
   in a dice-game? Up, down, a mere toying
      with a bringing-to-be? With destroying?

1887

On a Rainy Day

It can be told her on a day like this,
when a downpour has its way like this,
    when clouds rumble,
    when skies tumble,
on a sunless night-in-day like this.

Not a whisper will be known of this.
Nothing is as on its own as this.
    We two only,
    sad and lonely –
and the endless rain to witness this.
None else will the earth admit to this.

People all about are all unreal,
like the clatter of society's wheel.
    Eyes are linking,
    sweetness drinking,
as one heart the other heart can feel.
All else will the silent dark conceal.

To tell you this, my heart will not be shocked.
To say it, my own ear will not be blocked.
    Words will blend
    with tears, descend
till rain and wind hear all the speech of this,
and words have brimmed the heart of each with this.

Will anybody suffer, one soul smart,
if I set down the burden of my heart?
    If I whisper
    two words to her
in *Srabon*'s rain, in a room set apart –
it will not make the wide world stop or start!

And for a twelve-month to come after this,
with all the words and laughter after this,
    each tomorrow
    sadness, sorrow,
a world of people chasing over this –
so the words will fade, erasing this.

Today the wind blows quick and hard and fast,
the momentary lightning flashes past.
    Set apart
    deep in the heart,
now once the word – and not again of this,
in such a deep and heavy rain as this.

1888

Boundless Love

I have loved you a hundred ways, I think, a hundredfold,
    age after age in birth on birth untold.
Under your spell my heart has strung in song
    a necklace ever-new. You've worn it all along,
      age after age in birth on birth untold.

The more I hear the legend of long-ago love and pain,
    of tryst and parting between man and maiden,
the more I see shine through the endless stain
    of Time's dark night, your image, over and over again,
      as the North Star, with infinite memories laden.

Adrift, the pair of us, on a twinned love, we came
    from the source and heart of Time beyond beginning,
in countless lovers, we two playing our game,
    that now dear separation, now union sweet became –
      an old love in a robe of a new spinning.

Today that boundless love attains its final stage
    to lie heaped at your feet. Now all engage
within one love, all from the cosmic stage –
    the memory of all loves – joy, grief – all the heart's rage –
      the singing of every poet in every age.

1888

Cloud-Envoy

What year that's out of mind now, far away,
was it, on holy *Asharh*'s opening day,
when you set down your *Meghdut*, Poet? The echo
of clouds, down the dark line-ranks, bore the sorrow
of all who suffer parting's pain on Earth,
storing it deep in heaps in your song's depth.

At Ujjain's palace I don't know how dense
the clouds were on that day – or how intense
the reckless wind, the lightning's festival,
the thunder's note – I cannot tell at all.
The clouds' armed combat woke then, on that day,
the tears of separation that deep lay
within a pain-mist of a thousand years.
As though in one day all eternity's tears
till then suppressed, ran freely in your rhyme,
and tore apart the binding of old time,
to make that great verse sob.

                    On that day then
in every land did all far-travelling men
look up towards the clouds? Then each one turning
towards his loved one's home, a song of yearning,
hands folded – did they all together sing?
Were they intent to launch upon the wing
of a new cloud, unfettered, a love-word
brim-full of tear-mist? – so borne, to be spurred
to a far window where a lady lay

repining for her love? Her hair astray,
weeping, in faded dress, distraught she lies.

Poet, as day and night across the skies
they sought their lonely loved ones, did you send
their song in yours, far casting, to the world's end?
For in that way the Ganga river flows
and gathers in all waters as it goes
in *Srabon*, to be lost in the great sea.
So in that way the Himalayas see,
as from the stone chain of that prison-home
the heaven-clouds of *Asharh* freely roam
the endless sky, and so they sigh and breathe
vapour up from a thousand caves beneath,
in a vast cloud itself into the air,
that like desires free-roaming here and there,
all cluster at the peak, embrace and blend
in one, to claim the whole sky in the end.

How many hundred times, since that day ended,
has the time of the soft new rains descended?
Each monsoon since then has thickly scattered
raindrops on your poem, and freshly watered
its new quickening – soft shade laying out
of cloudlets in it, echoing the sky's shout
again throughout it, making the current run
of rhythm in it, like a quick river spun.

How many ages now, how many people,
sitting in their lonely homes in the feeble
light of a lamp, their dear companion gone,

as the *Asharh* dusk drags on and on
storm-wearied-out, to moonless, starless night,
have put the pain of loneliness to flight,
by your poem's soft and slow reciting?
I hear the voice of all of them alighting
at my ear, as if the rippling water
of ocean-waves.

On India's eastern border
I'm sitting in the green land of Bengal
where poet Joydev saw a shadow fall
of *tamal*-trees, green-dark, and far away,
when clouds had soaked the sky, one rainy day.

Today it's dark. On and on it rains.
A storming wind. All the forest complains
with arms upraised, and howls at the attack.
The lightning peeks out, tearing the cloud-rack
here and there with lacerating grin.

I sit alone, I'm reading *Meghdut* in
a dark closed house. My mind has broken out
of home, from land to land it's flying about,
carried on cloud-back. Amrakuta's peak,
now where the tumbling Reba waters seek
the Vindhya foothills, here and there agleam
along that narrow pebble-chafing stream,
now at the Vetravati river's side,
where Dasharna village seems to hide
in the shade of laden *jaam*-trees darkling,
fenced-in with the *ketaki*-flower's encircling,

where the village-birds in wayside-trees
chatter among the great trunks as they please,
making their nests in the rain! But by which river
a forest-girl looks out for the clouds' cover,
a lotus tired with cheek's heat tucked above
her ear, as she walks past the *juthi*-grove,
I do not know. Women who have not learned
tricks of the eyebrow, seeing with eyes upturned
a sky of massed cloud, these small-township wives,
into whose eyes the azure sky-shade dives,
who are they? By which mountain dark as cloud
does a nymph of the hills, under a shroud
of a fresh coolness, lose herself in wonder?
Suddenly in a downpour, wind and thunder,
she whisks about, clutching her clothes in fear,
and looks for a cave, exclaiming "Mother dear,
the top of the mountain's flying off, it seems!"
Where is Avanti, where Nivindhya's streams,
where in Shipra River does Ujjain peep
at its own glory? Pigeons are asleep
on rooves at midnight there, forgetting all
love's restlessness; but hearing the heart call,
in separation's fever women move
upon the road at night to meet their love,
in dark's thick cloak, as lightning flicks the air.
Where to north is Kurukshetra? Where
does Kankhal lie? There Ganga, Janhu's daughter,
laughs and frolics in the frothing water,
and teasing-playful, Gauri's frown ignoring,
lifts Shiva's locks into the moon's outpouring.

Just as a cloud is wafted by and past
this land and that, the heart arrives at last
at Alakā, its heaven, the one and all
of its desires. Beauty's original
is she who stays here, all without her lover,
lady most loved. Poet, to take me over
to Lakshmi's city of delight revealed –
who else but you in the immortal world!
It is Spring forever in a flower-garden,
a lotus blooms beside the lake's edge, golden,
as by a sapphire hill, in the constant moon,
with all the countless riches that festoon
a jewelled palace, yet alone, appears
a woman weeping separation's tears.
Through the open window see her lying,
like the moon's line in the east faint-dying,
slender along the bed. Your poem today
has shown at last my lonely heart the way
to free itself of its imprisonment.
Your spell has let me into the ascent
of separation's heaven. In night's keeping
stays the dear one, lonely, never sleeping,
in an eternal beauty to be found.

Again it's gone: the rain falls all around:
I see no end to it. Night's blind shadow
deepens alone. The wind out in the meadow
into an endless nowhere travels weeping.
A thought comes to me as I lie unsleeping:
who cursed us with a screen before our love?
Why should the mind weep as it looks above?

Why is love on its own way forestalled?
What man has been, by bodily form withheld,
to the imagined lake, and visited,
in sunless, jewel-lit half-light, that dear bed
of love's deep longing? Where all ways have led,
past all the hills and rivers of the world.

1890

To Ahalya

What did you dream of, Ahalya, set fast
in stone, while weary ages passed?
No holy fires burnt on where you stayed.
Sages had left that forest-shade.
Of Earth's mighty body you took a share –
then were you conscious of her great care?
In those stone depths did a few sensations
tell of the nursing mother's patience?
Her great silent pain, her sorrow, delight –
did they inform, as a dream might,
your sleeping soul? Day and night lakhs, crores
of life's blends and battles – her rages, tears, roars –
her joys and sadnesses never-ending –
her billions of travelling footsteps attending
each second – did you hear them? Did they break
your accursèd sleep? and so keep you awake
scarcely feeling, numb, brittle and blind?

Then were you able to sense in your mind
the great Mother's pain, untouched by sleep's ease?
Then on the day of the new Spring breeze
sweeping Earth's body with joyful fire,
did it caress you? A quickening desire
that a thousand different forms embraces
as it triumphs over desert-places,
that rose in anger to overthrow
your curse of a sterile stone form – did its blow
set life trembling in you again?

When night falls on the house of men
Earth drags weary bodies to rest.
So many lives sleep on her breast,
hard labour forgetting, under the sky
that stays awake . . . each sleeping sigh
from bodies relaxed, reaches Earth's heart.
That life-warmth on the Mother's part,
some touch of that did you assume?

Where she stays in her secret room,
behind a vivid curtain-net
of leaves and flowers (a language set
in coloured letters), and no sun feels,
from where in wealth and crop she steals
to enrich her brood – in that deep place
you slept so long in the Earth's embrace,
a forever cool night of oblivion.
Slumbering there at peace on and on
lakhs of tired lives on a dust-bed lie.
They wither and fall at the blink of an eye –
spent meteors and stars, exhausted flowers,
used deeds, tired joys, quenched sorrows, lost powers.

There with cool hands the Mother has purged
the stamp of hot sin. Today you emerged
Earth's newborn maiden, lovely, free
and innocent-open. Wordlessly
you gaze upon the morning's world.
The dew that once your stone empearled
at nightfall, now you thrillingly wear
in your long black knee-kissing hair.

The moss that so long covered you,
Earth's dark-green lovely mantle, new
continually in rains, moist-dense,
now offers at the Mother's expense
a garment made with her soft grace,
your naked beauty to embrace.

The world smiles its remembered smile.
You gaze at it transfixed – meanwhile
upon the dust-path of Time's chart,
retracing all its steps, your heart
is travelling far alone. And slowly
your earlier sense of things is wholly
felt again. The whole world, drawn
from all directions, depths, re-born
before you, has pressed close to see . . .
to stare amazed, transfixedly.

Beautiful mystery, woman-form bare,
bathed in a fresh earliness there –
as if, on a young stalk, a flower
from its leaf-cup shone in full power –
as if, from the first night, were drawn
up from oblivion's sea, the dawn.
Amazed you gaze at the Earth. It too
is silent as it faces you.
On mystery's great shore now is born
in the ever-knowing, a knowledge new.

1890

The Golden Boat

It's deep monsoon. The thunder-sky-clouds call.
I wait alone but with no hope at all.
    Now the paddy-harvest's over,
    brimming baskets stretch forever . . .
as the currents of the river cut and thrust and maul.
In harvest-time the rain began to fall.

On the bank in a small field I stay
alone. Across the stream's cross-purpose-play,
    I see the painting of a village
    in cloud-shadow. Trees and foliage
cluster in a dark ink-collage. It's early in the day.
In the field alone I sit and stay.

Who's that bringing his boat in, singing a song?
It seems as if I've known him all along.
    On the course back out he's starting,
    looking nowhere, and departing
in full sail. The waves break, parting, helpless in their throng.
It seems as if I've known him all along.

Friend, where are you off to, what far shore?
Turn and bring your boat in, just once more!
    Then go where you will, your bounty
    grant to whom you will in plenty –
but smiling for an instant, even, only take before
my golden paddy, coming to this shore.

Take however much you want aboard.
More yet? – No, I've given all my hoard.
    All that I was lost in, staying
      on the river's bank, delaying
long – all that in your boat laying, you have safely stored.
Now in your kindness take me too aboard.

No room, no room! The small boat, stacked today
even with my paddy's gold, is under way.
    In the *Srabon* sky forever
      clouds are darkly wheeling over
an empty and deserted river where I sit and stay.
The golden boat took all there was away.

1892

I Will Not Let You Go

The coach is at the gate. The autumn light
slowly turns still more intense and bright.
On the deserted country road dust strays
in the noon wind. A beggar-woman arrays
her rags, and tired and old, drops off to sleep
in an *ashwattha*'s shade – as if in deep
silence, a sunny night blazed all around.
Only in my home no rest's to be found.

The *puja* holiday's over, *Ashwin*'s past,
to a far place I must start back at last –
that place of work. Busy with rope and string
the servants are securing everything.
This room, that room echoes with shouts and cries.
The lady of the house, with brimming eyes,
feels at her heart a stony weight – but still,
no time for tears! Each second, all her skill
is spent in flying here and there, to manage
the lead-up to my leaving. The more luggage
the less it seems to her. I say, "Please, please!
These pitchers and these pictures – and all these
pots and pans and bottles and boxes, bedding –
what shall I do with all this? It's not heading
out with me! I'll take what I need
and leave the rest."
                         Nobody pays heed.
"If this or that's not needed, who can say?
It might be what you're looking for one day.

You won't know where to get it, take my advice,
in a strange place! The best *mugdal*, fine rice,
betel and *paan*; the lid of that urn shuts
on cake of molasses; a few dry coconuts;
some milk; there's mango pickle and mango candy;
two pots of mustard-oil will come in handy;
these phials and jars are medicines; now mind,
somewhere inside the pans some sweets you'll find –
and don't forget, you eat them, or eat my head!"
I saw that there was nothing to be said.
The load was all in, mountain-high. Then learning
what time it was, to my beloved turning,
I gazed at her dear face, and slowly said,
"So then, I'm off." At once she bowed her head
aside, and with her sari-scarf as screen,
she kept the inauspicious tears unseen.

My daughter's sitting by the door outside,
four years old, and much preoccupied.
She'd have bathed by now, another day.
I'd have seen the heavy eyelids weigh
with sleep, just as the mouth touched rice. And now
her mother lets her be. It's late. Yet how
can she be given bath or meal? So long,
a shadow sticking to my side, among
the leaving preparations, she looked on
with silent gaze. Now where her thoughts have gone,
as she's been sitting still here, who can know?
I said, "My little lady, I must go,"
and she replied with sad eyes and wan face,
"I will not let you go." And from her place

she did not stir, my arm she did not hold,
she did not stand in the door's way – but told
what her own heart insisted on, love's due.
"I will not let you go." But what to do?
The time was up – and I must be let gone.

My little daughter, O my simple one,
who do you think you are, where do you find
the strength to say it, the intrepid mind,
"I will not let you go" – ? Who in the world
can two such tiny hands keep back, withhold,
my proud-heart madam? Perched beside the door,
with whom will that small weary frame make war,
its strength all lying in a small fond heart!
With proper modesty one must impart
a wish in this world, timorously say,
"I do not want to let you go away."
Then who can say, "I will not let you go"?
Your childish mouth. Hearing it say so
and chuckling at the great proud words of love,
the world caught hold of me and dragged me off.
Still as a painting you stayed at your seat
beside the door. Your tears welled in defeat.
I went, wiping my eyes.

                    Along the road
both sides, I see the rich autumnal load
down-sway the crop-field as it basks in sun.
Rows of trees stand unconcerned, each one
gazing at its shade all day before
the highway. The full thrust of Ganga's bore

pierces Autumn. A white piece of cloud,
like a calf that mother's-milk-endowed,
new-born, handsome, rests contentedly,
is sleeping in the blue sky. As I see
the earth uncovered in the strong sun, bearing
itself out to the horizon, ever wearing
the tiring touch of age on age, I sigh.

What deep sorrow touches all the sky
and all the world! However far or near
I travel, this one mournful note I hear,
"I will not let you go." From the last end
of Earth, to where the furthest skies extend,
it sounds eternal in an infinite call,
'I will not – will not let you go.' So all,
"I will not let you go." Our Mother Earth
exclaims for all her very life is worth,
holding the slightest blade of grass to her,
"I will not let you go." Barely astir
at the lamp's lip, a flame is doomed and dying –
who saves it from the gulp of darkness, crying
as it is still tugged back to being, "No,"
a hundred times, "I will not let you go!"
It is the oldest word, the deepest cry
across the Earth and over heaven's sky,
within the universe that does not cease,
"I will not let you go." And still release
must come, alas, there is a letting-go,
there is a going. Has it not been so
since time without beginning? Eagerly
with arms outstretched upon destruction's sea,

and in creation's flow, with burning eyes,
and calling out, "No letting go!" all flies
on by, with a tremendous skimming motion,
and fills the Earth's shore with a crazed commotion.
The rear wave catches at the wave ahead,
"I'll not – not let you go!" Nothing is said
in answer, no one pays it any heed.

Today from everywhere around indeed
there sounds upon my ear incessantly
that world-heart-penetrating threnody
in my young daughter's voice. As if a child
announced it, the unknowing word of the world.
For always what it finds it will let slip,
and yet it does not loosen that tight grip,
but still like one whose love is whole and proud,
a girl of four years old, it calls out loud,
"I will not let you go." And tearful-eyed,
wan-faced, at every instant with its pride
in tatters, love will not accept defeat –
but chokingly, rebelliously repeat,
"I will not let you go." However often
it has to lose, it will never soften,
but still demand, "How can it ever be
the one I love will go away from me?
Can the world hold anything at all
as sharp as my desire, as powerful,
as infinite? Can anything compare?"
And with such perfect pride it will declare,
"I will not let you go!" At once it sees
a speck of dry dust on a puff of breeze,

its heart's delight escape – away that flies.
And so it weeps with bowed head; and it lies
like an uprooted tree on the earth now.
And still love says, "God will not break his vow.
I have his special promise, signed and sealed,
a warrant of eternal right." So steeled,
and standing proudly now before the face
of death omnipotent, with tender grace
of lissom beauty, love says – with what pride –
"Death, you are not real." Death laughs. World-wide
this ever-living love, disturbed by death,
draws far and near, like a tear-mist's breath
over sad eyes, in a tremulous haze.
Hope, that's out of hope and weary, lays
its sorrow-mist upon the world. I see
today, as if it were in front of me,
about the universe, a fruitless binding
of two unknowing arms, forever winding
in silent sad embrace. Cast on the stream,
all-still upon its restless flow, a dream
of some rain-tearful cloud – a shadow falls.

And so it is that so much eagerness calls
in the trees' rustling now; as at midday
in idle carelessness warm breezes play
tricks with dry leaves. In a slow parade
time takes its time to lengthen out the shade
of an *ashwattha*-tree. A singing stirs
within the meadow of the universe,
a country flute that weeps to utter there
infinity's note. And she seems not to care,

the listening lady of the Earth, beside
the Ganga seated, hair loose; far and wide
the corn-field stretches where she is at rest;
a sari-sash is drawn up on her breast
of sunlit-yellow-gold; and her two eyes
absorbed, are fixed upon the far blue skies;
and she says not a word. So wan her face –
my daughter, four years old, is at her place
beside the door. So silent, sad her air;
a part of the place itself, as she sits there.

1892

Swinging

I and my soul will take part in a game of death
tonight.
Skies louring, a stormy-showering,
now the downpour's overpowering.
On a wave of the world my raft is hurled –
out on the deep no dream, no sleep
tonight.

Dear one, what a wild uproar of sea-wind-sky!
Swing the swing.
Now it's jostling, now it's chortling,
from the back a mad storm's hurtling –
a screaming and teeming of child-demons –
as lunatics cry in a drunkards' hell-sky.
Swing the swing.

Today my soul is awake and alert at its place
in my breast.
A fearful shivering, a joyful quivering –
now clenching, now itself delivering –
fierce and tight in the heart's delight –
a shy advancing – my soul is dancing
in my breast!

Ah, for so long on the bed I cosseted her
with such care.
Lest hurt unsettle, or sorrow startle,
every day and night too gentle

with flowers I spread a bridal bed;
   I tucked her away each night, each day
      with such care.

For so long have I caressed her, kissed her eyes
      all-tenderly –
   and soft tales told her, and pet-names called her,
   my head by hers, with dear words lulled her –
soft would I croon love-songs by the moon –
   a wealth of charms I set in her arms
      all-tenderly.

On that happy indolent bed my soul seems tired,
      under a spell.
She does not stir at my touch's spur,
   her wreaths lie heavily on her;
together seep day's light, night's sleep;
   the heart's to a numb detachment come,
      under a spell.

Lavishing sweetness I seem to be losing the bride
      I long for and seek.
   All about my quick eyes scout –
   the bridal lamp is nearly out –
dead flowers drift free. In a deep sea
   of dreams I founder. Who is it, I wonder,
      I long for and seek?

I have decided we will begin a new game
      tonight.
   Side by side, so close-allied,

holding the ropes, death's swing we'll ride –
with laughter raucous the storm will rock us –
I and my soul in Swinging-Day role
      tonight!
    Swing the swing.
    Swing the swing.
On the great sea a gale will spring.
I have my bride back, everything
is well. Destruction's manic ding
wakes my beloved. My veins sing
a song of waves, a shattering.
    Within, without, all's deafening.
    Tresses fly, a sash takes wing,
    forest-garlands spin and fling
    wild in the wind – small, large, a string
    of bangles jangle, madly ring.
    Swing the swing.

O storm come and so remove
the veil of my soul-bride, my love,
and strip away the covering.
    Swing the swing.
Face to face my soul and I
unafraid and no more shy
will know, will touch each other, cling
heart to heart in passion's Spring.
    Swing the swing.
Groom and bride, dreams swept aside,
two mad people come outside.
    Swing the swing.

1893

No Destination

Beautiful lady, how far are we sailing on?
Where is the shore your golden boat will put in?
    Dear one, strange and lovely lady,
smiling you say nothing to me –
what is in your thoughts I do not know.
    Silently you indicate
    the endless sea in restless spate.
Far in the west the sun is setting low.
What do we seek, where is it that we go?

Lady beyond my knowing, speak if I ask –
where the pyre of day is lit on the bank of dusk,
    a blinding fire on water swirls,
    and the firmament melts and spills,
where the eyes of the Nymph of Directions brim with tears
                                          and fill –
    is it there that you reside,
    the wave-resounding sea beside,
at the foot of a cloud-kissed sunset hill?
You smile and look at me, unspeaking still.

For ever the wind exhales its gusts and sighs.
A blind passion roars on the high seas.
    Deep blue waters shift and stir,
    on no side can I see a shore,
a weeping floods the world in a wild swaying.
    On that the golden boat floats by,
    on that falls light of the dusk sky,

in that this silent smile ... why, nothing saying?
I do not know the game that you are playing.

When first you called out "Who will come?" I rose
on that new morning, glancing at your eyes.
    Your arms, flung out in front, embraced
    an endless ocean to the west;
a fleeting light like hope on the deep rolled.
    "What new life is out there?" then
    I asked, and boarded. And again,
"What dream of hope grows there in fruit of gold?"
You looked at me, you smiled, and no word told.

Since then the clouds have risen, the sun has come,
now riotous waves, and now a picture of calm.
    Hours pass, a puff of air comes soon,
    somewhere the golden boat moves on,
I see the sun upon the west low-lying.
    I dare to ask one question more –
    is there soothing death in store,
is all let go, lost in a dark untying?
You smile, and raise your eyes, without replying.

Dark night will come with wings outspread to mask
the golden light, even now, in this sky-dusk.
    Only your fragrance can I sense,
    and hear the water's turbulence.
Your locks lift up in the wind, caressing me.
    Heart and body spent and gone,
    my urgent call still carries on,

"Come close and touch me, dear – where can you be?"
No word. That silent smile I cannot see.

1893

Song of the City

The green Earth, fresh and peaceful too,
with its hem of shining blue,
where has it departed to,
    a world so fine and fair?
The sky's raptures of light and ease,
the lonely cool shade of the trees,
the solemn murmuring of the bees,
    and I have sailed to – where?
There is the city, the human jungle,
houses, highways in a vast tangle,
so many shops have hung out their shingle,
    so much noise and unrest!
Sense and nonsense in a blind muddle
fog the Earth, the heavens befuddle,
sun-hot dust flies up in a spiral,
    the great sky is distressed.
Everything's part of a smash-and-crash,
joining and parting in a flash,
not a trace stays, but at a dash
    into death's sea it's gone.
Callous laughter, pitiful crying,
cruel remarks, an eager trying,
high pride, service meek-replying,
    so it goes on and on.
Not for a second does anything stay
or look back on its outward way,
in dark and light, in night and day
    careering on without stop.

Greedy at heart the young and old
chase a dream, for they would hold
a deer, dancing in dazzling gold,
    and snare it, tie it up.
As if a sacrificial fire
erupted from its pit, to spire
in a consuming high desire,
    a wavering trunk of flame!
Men and women troop to their goal,
to the fire's mouth with their bowl,
to break it and pour down the whole
    of life, each one the same.
To a primal Power they offer faith,
attached to golden-coloured death,
on every side they give their breath,
    their bones, their blood they give.
The world-flame snarls in smoke, to stun
the heavens on high, and terribly run
through pores of space, and make the sun
    and moon turn fugitive.
All the winds turn mad and swarm
about the bright flame's flickering form,
puffing out breath so wildly warm,
    sobbing, unsatisfied.
As if on piteous wings outspread,
desperate to get nestlings fed,
to a forest burnt to the last shred,
    bird-mothers came and cried.
Brahmin, *shudra*, great and small,
kshatriya, *vaishya*, one and all,

a terrible fire-ritual
    of life have started up.
Seeing this great burning game,
like insects they desire the same,
to sacrifice their body's frame
    to the last life-drop!
O city, your great foaming cup
of heady wine is bubbling up
and brimming over, yet I'll sup
    from it, myself forsaking!
O stony nurse whose charge and care
is man, I'll travel to your fair,
we'll pass the night together there,
    a drunken revelry making!
Crowds and crowds in circling streams,
a loveless closeness swarms and teems —
and I shall smash my hidden dreams
    among them, keeping none.
Peace to me is of no avail,
I'll rise and triumph, fall and fail,
and I shall catch a comet's tail
    and spread my arms to the sun!
Fate plays new games by the hour,
helpful, harmful, sweet and sour:
whatever it lies in my power
    to take to myself, to feel —
now joy, now sorrow is in store —
at times on poetry I'll soar,
at times in deep prose brush the floor —
    spinning on the Big Wheel!

I'll take the trumpet of victory –
I the unquiet, the wildly free –
and faced with impossibility
    I shall carry the day.
With pity I shall never bleed –
I'll grab to satisfy my need –
and from another's mouth indeed
    I'll wrench the food away!
I will come to know that all
the Earth is my foot's pedestal;
a robber's patch, a great king's hall,
    these two I know are one.
The world's a pinch of snuff, no more,
I'll rob the harvest of its store,
and as I seek to gather more,
    I'll let the free horse run!
Newly hungering, thirsting new,
works and projects still to do,
the book of life as I go through
    flicks each fresh page over.
The way I race is winding, bending,
no beginning and no ending,
now ascending, now descending,
    past sea, hill and river.
A night-bird I, without a nest,
ever ahead, ahead the quest,
and you too running without rest,
    goddess, seek to blind me.
Lakshmi, I do not implore you,
worship at your feet, adore you –

I shall take the prize before you,
    trussing you up behind me!
Human life is quickly over,
honour, wealth and famed endeavour,
they are trusty servants never,
    Time's stream waits for none.
Then for the few days you are able,
with the trials and with the trouble
of the tremendous ferment of people . . .
    fill up life's bowl, pour on.

1895

Chitra

You are here in a world-exuberance of forms,
        form-fleeting lady.
With a million lights in the blue sky gleaming,
with a quick delight in the garden blooming,
in the light-step thrill of a going-and-coming,
        far-restless lady.
Jangling anklets sound in the distant sky,
in the slow breeze a hair-fragrance wafts by;
deep in the cosmos dances magically
        many a melody.
In how many colours, worked in what gold-thread,
in tune and cadence and in song-notes spread,
in so many books, by so many voices read,
        your stories' medley!
You are here in a world-exuberance of forms,
        form-fleeting lady.

Within the heart none else, but one alone,
        heart-dwelling lady.
The tearful eye can see but one lotus;
within there is but one dream; in the boundless
sky of mind, one moon, in night that's endless,
        is sailing, lady.
Here is the mighty ending, peace that's shoreless;
a devotee performs the rite of service;
no time, no land – a lightning motionless
        is falling, lady.
There is a glory that is yours, so clear,

so deep, a blueness of the eye is here,
a smile that like the dawn is far and near,
    soft-smiling lady!
Within the heart none else, but one alone,
    heart-dwelling lady.

1985

Urvashi

Not, mother, not daughter, not bride, woman-form of all beauty,
    Paradise's Urvashi!
When day's tired body, in gold sari, dusk-touches the meadow,
you will light no lamp for the house in evening's shadow.
To no bridal bed, eyes down, in a timid politeness
do you step, heart beating, with a smile of shy sweetness
    in night's silent lateness.
Like the risen dawn, its veil abandoning,
    is your unafraid being.

Like a bloom without stalk, born of itself entirely,
    when did you blossom, Urvashi?
In the first of Spring's morning you rose from the labouring
                  ocean,
in right hand a nectar jar, in left a pot of poison.
Like a great serpent that is calmed by a spell's saying,
its million bristling hoods at your feet laying,
    the vast sea's waves are lying.
Like the white *kunda*-flower the king of gods praised in its purity
    is your sheer beauty!

Were you never a small child, a bud, a flower in infancy,
    ever-youthful Urvashi?
Under the dark sea in whose room with exciting
gems and pearls did you play, on your own alone sitting?
In whose lap did you sleep, in a chamber of the deep, the waves'
                  carol

nearby as you smiled, your face lit on the bed of coral
    by the flash of jewel on jewel?
You awoke in the world already with youth's power,
    at once in full flower.

Age upon age the world's sweetheart, you and you only,
    ravishing Urvashi!
Sages break in mid-trance, to lay at your feet their merit –
struck by your side-glance, the three worlds dance in spirit –
heady with your fragrance, the winds hurtle about their blind
                          journey –
the poet whirls around, spellbound, like a bee drunk with honey,
    uttering wild harmony!
Where you are anklet-bells ring, a sari is flying,
    and lightning volleying!

In the hall of the gods when you dance in a surge of ecstasy,
    O quick wave, Urvashi,
clusters of billows of the sea go dancing in rhythm,
corn-tips thrill as the Earth's sari strays among them,
from your necklace stars in the sky cascade down-slipping –
at once a man's heart is lost in wonder, as if sleeping,
    but his bloodstream is leaping!
On the horizon your dress streams out in abandon,
    unschooled – unruled one!

In the dawning-place of the sky the sun forms – you are She,
    world-bewitching Urvashi!
Tears of the cosmos stream over and wash your body,
with the heart's blood of three worlds your feet are made ruddy;

with hair loose, all naked, you have set your foot's lightness
where all the desires of the world have their flowering-impetus,
    as, lotus upon lotus –
for ever you frolic throughout the heart's heaven,
    O dream-companion!

Now hear all the earth and sky weeping for you bitterly,
    hard-of-heart Urvashi!
Will the world see again the gift of the original far age?
Will you rise again with wet hair from the deep vast surge?
When the first form shines out in the first morning's keeping,
in the violent gaze of the world all your body will be weeping
    with water dropping!
Suddenly the world's great ocean will drive its wave-water
    to new songs of wonder.

She will not return, she will not return . . . where the moon's
                                        majesty
    has set, lives Urvashi!
And so today at the delight of the Spring-season,
whose sigh of eternal parting is breathed in with that passion?
On full-moon night when all ten directions are brimming with
                                        laughter,
why should memory play a distressed flute, ever softer,
    many tears falling after?
Yet hope wakes and lives in a sob of the soul's knowing,
    O all-free Being!

1895

Life's Monarch

Deepest-of-all,
within my soul's depth now you fall,
    and have you slaked your thirst?
With a thousand streams of pain and pleasure
I have filled your cup's full measure,
wringing my heart with a pressure cruel –
    kneading it to grape-burst!
Scent on scent and hue on hue,
so many songs and rhythms too –
it is your wedding-bed with these
    I made, weaving away.
Melting, melting the gold of desire,
I have fashioned from the fire
images that stay ever-new,
    for your moment's play.

You have welcomed me. What hopes
    you had I cannot tell.
Monarch of Life, did you delight
in my dawn and in my night,
in my labour, in my play,
    where you lonely dwell?
In winter, autumn, monsoon, spring,
all the songs my soul would sing –
alone upon your throne, did you
    discern that melody?
Was there a garland for your wearing

in the flowers of my mind's bearing?
In the woodland of my youth
   did your heart roam free?

What do you see in my soul, dear friend?
   Do your eyes not harden
at my failings, falterings, flaws –
   or do they grant pardon?
Days and nights of worship bereft,
so often the deity has left,
as flowers-of-offering pine, unplucked
   in a lonely garden.
You tuned a *veena* to your way:
ever more slackly its strings play.
O Poet, the song that you composed,
   how shall I ever sing?
Going to water your flowery glade
I fell asleep under the shade.
In the dusk with brimming tears
   water now I bring.

Is it all at an end, my lord and friend,
   all that there was of mine?
Sleep's blind power, the wakening hour –
   the song, life, beauty fine?
Is life's bower to fill with light
that was the trysting-place of night?
Loosened is the embrace of arms,
   my kisses have lost their wine.
Then break up the court of today

and bring new forms, a new array
of beauty. I the ever-old
   you take again as new.
Bring me within life's bond. I pray,
   the wedding-tie renew.

1896

Night and Dawn

In moonlight in the passionate night in the garden-bower
I held up to your lips the flashing wine of youth's rich hour.
    You looked at my eyes, lazily
    you took the foaming glass from me,
and with lips moist with kisses' promise, drank it smilingly,
in moonlight in the passionate night of love's ecstasy.
    The veil at first about your head,
    I drew it off, and it was shed;
your lotus-tender hand I took, and to my heart it wed;
your two eyes closed in feeling thought, and not a word was said.
    The knot of your hair I unbound,
    the tresses falling loosely round,
    your lowered face then came to rest
    (what joy was mine) against my chest –
you laughed to feel the rain of my caresses in full shower,
in moonlight in the passionate night of our love's sweet power.

In windswept dawn upon the silent river-bank today
your bath is over, dressed in white you slowly make your way.
    A basket held in your left hand,
    you pluck the flowers from river-land . . .
a far flute sounds a dawn-song in a temple, light and grand,
in windswept dawn beside the silent Ganga as you stand.
    A vermilion mark is born,
    lady, where the *sindoor*'s drawn;
on your wrist a conch-shell bangle, a slim moon, is worn.
In such a form of loveliness do you appear at dawn!
    At night in the beloved's part

you came, the empress of my heart;
now as a smiling goddess decked
you come at dawn. In deep respect
my head is lowered. At a distance now I stand and stay,
in windswept dawn upon the silent river-bank today.

1896

A hundred years from now
who are you, turning to this poem's page
with eager brow,
a hundred years from now!
A tiniest morsel of delight
of this new Spring,
a morning flower, a birdsong trill, a snatch
of colouring –
can I bespeak it to your hand, still fresh
in my love's vow,
a hundred years from now?

Some time for sure   the south-facing door
you'll open, and in fancy's play
you'll sit where you are,   yet see from afar
a day, one day
a hundred years ago –
when drifting down   from some heaven blown
came showers of delight,   deep, deep to alight –
to the heart of the cosmos they go;
when a fresh *Phalgun* day,   madly astray,
of all restraint free,
soars on wild wings,   and pollen-scent brings,
as out on a spree
a south wind of youth   touches the Earth
with colourful glow,
a hundred years ago.

A poet awoke,   cast off the yoke,
        and let a song flow –
so on that day   with so much to say,
with words like flowers   he drew on his powers
        to shape and to show
            a day, one day
            a hundred years ago.

    A hundred years from now
whose are the new songs that inside your homes
            you all allow?
    Who is the poet-minstrel? Let me send
    a vital greeting from the Spring today
            to that poet's hand.
    Let my Spring song in your Spring day
            a moment stand –
within your heart-beat, in a young bee humming,
            a rustling bough,
        a hundred years from now.

1896

Mother Bengal

In sin and saintliness, to rise and fall,
in joy and sorrow let your offspring grow.
Do not home-nestle them, O fond Bengal,
eternal infants all – but let them go.
To this or that land send them to discover
a place of their own seeking – do not shroud
these goody-goody children under cover,
their every step of freedom disallowed.
Let them risk all, themselves their only aid,
with good and bad to tussle in the fray.
Take up your reedy sons, that pious brigade,
and send them homeless out on a hard way.
  Seventy million children, mother hen,
  you shelter as Bengalis – not as men.

1896

Woman

Woman, created not by God alone,
man moulds you too! Out of his own heart
he proffers beauty. As the poets intone,
their golden similes clothe you with their art;
the artist an immortal form devises,
according a new greatness, a new shine;
such colour, fragrance, ornament arises –
the pearl comes from the sea, gold from the mine,
and woodland flowers of Spring to beautify –
and insects die so that your feet are dyed.
Man decorates you, veils you, makes you shy,
till you are precious, hidden, rarefied.
   All lit up by his longing, his elation –
   you are half woman, half imagination.

1896

Black Time

Slowly, slowly though the day has gone,
    all songs have stopped, as at a sign made dumb;
the endless sky holds no companion;
    with weariness the body is overcome;
and terror tells its mute prayer on and on,
    and everywhere a veil is over things. –
Yet, bird, even now, O my bird,
    sightless one, lightless one, do not fold your wings.

This is no forest leaf-reverberant,
    it is the ocean's snake hissing and rearing;
no arbour with the *kunda*-flower's light vibrant;
    it is a roaring wave and foam wild-shearing.
Where is that bank with leaf and flower exuberant,
    that nest, that to its branch so firmly clings? –
Yet, bird, even now, O my bird,
    sightless one, lightless one, do not fold your wings.

Still ahead is that far endless blackness,
    the sun sleeps on behind the sunset-hill.
The universe checks all its breath in blankness,
    and counts the hours, alone and silent-still.
A thin, curved moon has swum the shoreless darkness,
    and on the far horizon rests and swings. –
Yet, bird, even now, O my bird,
    sightless one, lightless one, do not fold your wings.

Stars above gesticulating, facing
   down at you, stare at you beneath.
From below a hundred waves are racing
   up at you, of impatient death.
Who are calling, hands together placing,
   "Come"? The sad word from a far shore rings. –
Yet, bird, even now, O my bird,
   sightless one, lightless one, do not fold your wings.

There is no fear, no heartfelt doting tie.
   There is no hope, that plays tricks with the hours.
There are no words, no futile tears to sigh.
   There is no home, no making of lantern-flowers.
There are only wings, the great yard of the sky
   painted black. No sign of dawn it brings. –
Yet, bird, even now, O my bird,
   sightless one, lightless one, do not fold your wings.

1897

Forgive

Dearest, for my loving you,
　　I beg you to forgive, forgive.
A timid bird came to your cage;
　　don't shut it out, but let it live.
What's mine cannot stay at my side,
my reckless heart I will not hide;
you hide it then – with all inside
　　your heart, a powerless girl forgive.

Dearest, if you cannot love,
　　still forgive love, still forgive.
My friend, to greet a helpless girl,
　　no twinkling or amused look give.
I'll pick myself up, run away,
I'll burn in shame, in night I'll stay,
my heart's raw pain to lull, allay.
　　Dear, an unlucky girl forgive.

Dearest, if you should love me,
　　a torrent of joy forgive, forgive!
I'll float free on a loving tide –
　　then with a queen's prerogative,
I'll overpower you and thrill.
(Don't smile, my lord.) And then I will,
a goddess, your desires fulfil.
　　Now a vain girl forgive, forgive!

1897

Dream

From the ends of Earth
to seek my first love in a former birth
I had adventured, in the land of dream,
in Ujjain city, by the Shipra stream.
  I sought her in that place,
  lodhra-dusted her face,
  in her hand's display
  a lotus of love's play,
  and nestling at her ear
  a *kunda*-flower, and near
  above, lying in her hair,
  a *kurubak*-bloom set there.
  Sash-fastened, over all
  her body is let fall
  a crimson dress; below,
  where her feet softly go,
  anklet-bells half-ring.

It was in the Spring
that I had strayed that day
from a great distance, finding out the way.

In Shiva's temple, the great God of Time,
the *arati*-service sounds in a deep chime.
A row of shops, deserted . . . on a dark hall
above, a ray of evening is let fall.

The path is narrow, winding;
my dear one's house is lonely, hard of finding.
On the door conch and disc are styled;
on either side there, cared for as a child,
a *neepo* sapling grows; in sombre pride
on a white entrance-pillar at each side
a lion-figure sits.

Returning home
my dear one's doves now to the roof-top come.
A peacock sleeps deep on a bar of gold.

A burning lamp in her hand's hold,
slowly my love, my Malwa girl, comes down.
It seems a Lakshmi of the dusk is shown
with evening star, upon the garden-stair.
Her *kumkum* scent, the incense tang of her hair
exhale their restless breaths all over me.
In her loose dress, on her left breast I see
a leaf drawn in the paste of sandalwood.
She seemed to be an idol there that stood
in the quiet dusk, the city bustle over.

Seeing me her lover
slowly she set the lamp down at the door
and came and stood before me, and no more
than this her sad eyes asked, without a sound,
taking my hand in hers – "Are you well, friend?"
And I was going to speak, looking upon
her face, but there were no words, all had gone.

That language now was lost to me, and neither
person now recalled the name of either,
as we gazed at each other and wondered long,
and from unblinking eyes the tears fell strong.

So long we thought, beneath the entrance-trees!
I knew not when or by what magic ease
her soft fine hand had ventured out and hid
in my right hand, but only that it did,
like an evening bird seeking its nest.
At length her face, into this my breast,
like a bent-stem lotus lowered slowly.
Breath on breath, fervent, melancholy,
joined as one.

    The darkness of the night
took Ujjain out of time and out of sight.
    In the wild wind
when was it that the entrance-lamp went blind?
    By the Shipra river,
in Shiva's temple, *arati* was over.

1897

Year's End

From the North-East cloud-stacks race in blindly,
        unchecked, unbound,
in bamboo at the village-edge *kajol* darkens –
        rain sweeps the ground
in sheets, the year is out now, *Chaitra*'s over,
        night is near,
my heart is set to sing the very last song
        of the old tired year.

Cows raise their heads and trot, a farmer runs,
        the field's stained grey,
the timid boats dip sail at once, come in
        on the river's way.
The frayed-cloud West is livid with the glow
        of a red eye –
and flocks of scared birds race in flight as lightning
        slices the sky.

Strike, strike with sharper attack the *veena*'s strings,
        raise high its song –
and in that onslaught let the heart storm forth
        plentiful, strong.
Rush with a tempest's passion, Song, rise high
        on the sky's far way –
and let the thin pale leaf, on a great breath
        fly away, die away.

In a roaring of joy and tears – where fear's mad howl
      is one with gladness –
tying its anklets, let a storm of the Spring
      dance in its madness!
To the throb and beat of a sari-hem's whirl and flail,
      let the year pass,
and all its futile gleanings fly off and perish
      like dust like grass.

I have opened the door – O rain and storm of the sky
      come to my breast
and take my heart, a conch-shell, mightily sound it,
      rouse it from rest,
and pierce the sky with a wonderful proclamation
      of victory-rage –
and wake in the soul a bare, austere satisfaction,
      as of a sage.

That full deep tone, like the *Veda*-songs of old
      so rich in sound,
let it come from the whole heart in a moment,
      in pure form found.
No sorrow, no bliss, no shame, no ancient grievance,
      no shudder of fear
is there – but the victory-peal of a life new-bathed,
      bright and clear.

O new one, come, heaping the heavens, O fill them
      over and over –
extinguish all in a great layered array,
      in deep dense cover.

Suddenly veiling all in a swift second
        hide all away
and for a time, black-terrible in your dark depths,
        O calm one, stay.

Your gesture is as the lightning's glance beneath
        a thunderous scowl,
your song, as if through all the holes in the sky
        came the wind's howl,
your rain, charging at thirst, drives into it
        with all its might,
your quiet brings the far-spreading sleeping solemn
        silent black night.

This time you did not come on Spring's love-wave
        kissing the flowers,
this time you did not come with the gossiping birds –
        praise be yours!
Like a king you have come with chariot-wheels of thunder,
        brave, proud, you are he,
with a Word of thunder we hear or hear not. To you
        be victory!

Indomitable, inexorable, merciless, new,
        strong in your ease,
just as fruit scattering the dead flowers about
        its own way frees,
and ripping away the old leaves, finds its form
        all beautiful-new –
so in your great and full power you appear.
        I bow to you.

Dark, tireless, terrible, loving, ever-vivid –
    to you I bow.
Great hero new-born, what you bring with you
    you do not know.
Your flying banner is the burning sunbeam
    through clouds descending.
I glance up, suppliant, at its words, but gain
    no understanding.

Prince, smiling, draw your bow, and let it twang
    with its charged sound –
may the breast's ribs be pierced – that resonance
    within be found.
O youth, take up your noble victory-trumpet,
    issue your call –
we will stand up, and rush outside, and offer
    life and all.

We will not look back, to languish in chains, all cheerless,
    not count the hours,
not glance aside, not quibble of this and that –
    free travellers!
At once we'll drink the frothy madness of death
    till the throat be filled –
till all the shames of a weak and narrow life,
    all, all, we yield.

The stain of merely passing through life's day,
    the basket of shame,
as night after night a closed room is smoke-blackened
    in a lamp's small flame,

the tug of profit and loss, the minutest reckoning –
    distrust and brawl –
enough of it, this breaking life into splinters
    and squandering all!

The path humanity takes in terrible silence
    unendingly
O keep me by it – and the vast form of the ages
    I will see.
Like a hawk suddenly tear me from a mud-pool,
    like a hawk raise
and set me down, now face-to-face with great Death
    in lightning's blaze.

Throw me away then, grind me to dust, what you will –
    shatter my wings.
The stolen leaf, the fallen flower, the snapped branch,
    your swift playthings –
where all the idle leavings of your cruel theft
    at last have gone,
throw me into that land of endless darkness
    and oblivion.

The rain streams on, in a plot of sugar-cane shoots,
    without stop or stay.
From dark to dark the day in deeps of cloud
    has passed away.
A calm is come. The crickets chirp. Earth's fragrance
    comes pouring by.
At an open window I offer the year's last song
    to the night sky.

1899

Love-Tryst

He slept by Mathura's city wall, Upagupta the monk.
    The city's lamps were all blown out,
      the doors were closed, and all about
the *Srabon* sky was quite without its stars – in dense cloud sunk.

Whose foot, with tinkling anklet-bells, against his chest now flies?
    The heavy dream that lay upon
      his sleeping eyes, at once is gone . . .
and now a lamp's light glows down on those beautiful merciful
                           eyes!

A high-class hussy, in folly of youth, to a tryst was on her way.
    With jangling ornaments arrayed,
      her form a fine blue sash displayed –
but the tap of her foot on a body made Vasavadatta stay.

Lamp in hand, a light complexion first she looked upon:
    a youthful, calm and smiling face,
      eyes radiant with mercy's grace,
a fair-skinned brow from which a trace of moon's serenity shone.

Shyly now she looked at him, and sweetly then she said,
    "Young man, if I ask you to
      come back home with me, pray do:
the ground is very hard, and you deserve a softer bed!"

"Beautiful lady," said the monk and tenderly replied,
    "to your bower tonight I may

not come. Continue on your way.
But I will find another day to hurry to your side."

Suddenly a storm flashed fire, its huge mouth unlocking.
 She shook with fear, while in the wind
 a conch-shell of destruction dinned . . .
as mockingly the lightning grinned, and thunder laughed,
 sky-shocking.

. . . .

The year's round is not over. It is dusk in the Spring.
 Flowers bloom in an eager breeze
 on branches of the wayside trees;
while *bakul, parul,* tube-rose please the garden of the king.

Flute-tunes play from far away in raptures on the air.
 The town has gone off, one and all,
 to Madhubon's flower-festival.
The silent moon is smiling full on the lonely city there.

In the moonlight all alone the monk is walking past.
 Up above him, in tree-cover,
 a *kokil* calls, over and over –
has the tryst-night for the lover come around at last?

Holding his staff he crossed the city to the outer wall.
 At the moat's edge he stood where
 a mango-grove makes dark the air.
What woman's body is it there that has been let fall?

Riddled terribly with smallpox, it has been thrown clear,
    ink-black with disease's hand,
    out beyond the city's land
by residents who cannot stand that poisonous body near.

The monk sat down and in his lap her inert head he cradled.
    To dry lips he gave water there,
    and touched her head and said a prayer,
and smoothed cool sandal-paste on where her body was so
                        raddled.

A *kokil*'s calling, blossoms are falling in the wild moonlight.
    "Who are you, dear kind one?" said she.
    "Vasavadatta," then said he,
"at last the time has come to be, and I am here tonight!"

1899

Karna and Kunti: A Dialogue

Karna   By the holy Ganga I revere
the sun at dusk. Of the charioteer
Abhirath and Radha the true son,
Karna is my name. Respected one,
good mother, tell me who you are, I pray.

Kunti   My son, on your first and earliest day,
to introduce you to the world you see,
one there was indeed – and I am she,
Now today casting off all shame,
I have come to let you know my name.

Karna   Lady of grace, from your lowered gaze
a light descends, as if the sunlight's rays
upon a mountain's snow, melting my heart.
There comes a tone of voice, to wake and start
a pain of unmatched beauty, seeming as if
it came upon my ears from a past life,
to find me now. Unknown lady, say
by what strange bond, in what mysterious way
is my birth linked to you!

Kunti   Have patience yet
my son. Now let the sun's divinity set.
Before I speak let night-time's darkness grow.
Now I am telling you – O hero, know
that I am Kunti.

Karna   Kunti! Arjun's mother!

Kunti   Yes, knowing that is who I am, no other,
do not despise me! I remember still
at Hastina the test of weapon-skill.

You entered the arena steadily,
young as the early sun, that gradually
brightens the eastern star-sky, sure and certain.
Of all the women then behind the curtain,
who was that unfortunate woman who
could not speak out, and yet in whose heart grew
a desperate hunger for love? By a thousand snakes
kept alive, that pain ever wakes.
Whose eyes blessed and covered your body with kisses?
That was Arjun's mother – and so this is.
When Kripa asked your father's name and said,
with a scornful laugh, "He who is not bred
of kings, to challenge Arjun may not dare" –
your red lowered face was silent, you stood there –
then burning in the harsh glow of that shame,
which poor woman's heart was all aflame?
Arjun's mother. Then let him be praised,
son Duryodhan, since at once he raised
Karna to Anga's throne. Praise be to him!
Your coronation made my two eyes swim
with tears – as if on your own head they spilled.
Now into the arena, radiant-thrilled,
came Adhirath the charioteer. A crowd
milled round, all curious; your head you bowed –
still wet from its anointing – and all decked
in your new kingly robes, paid deep respect
to the old charioteer, calling him Father.
The Pandava supporters, with cruel laughter,
all cried out "Shame!" O bright jewel, from the side
who blessed you as a hero, bursting with pride?
It was Arjun's mother – it was I.

Karna	Gracious lady, I honour you! But why,
	mother of kings, have you come here alone?
	I am a Kaurava general.
Kunti	My son –
	something I beg – let it not be in vain.
Karna	You beg – of me! Whatever you ordain
	I'll lay it at your feet – except for this:
	my life's true duty, and my manliness.
Kunti	I have come to take you.
Karna	Take me where!
Kunti	Into my thirsting heart, a mother's care.
Karna	In five sons you are blessed and fortunate.
	My origin is indeterminate.
	An unimportant king – what place for me?
Kunti	At the head and top of all my sons shall be
	your seat – the eldest son's.
Karna	But with what right?
	For these have held and lost an empire's might.
	How can I take one part in their full share
	of the great richness of your motherly care?
	It is no dice's stake, for bartering,
	a mother's heart. Nor is it a thing
	to be obtained by force. It is God-given.
Kunti	My son, one day you came to this lap's haven
	by the right of God. Now by that same right
	come with pride, come with a heart that's light,
	to take your place, with all your brothers near,
	in a mother's lap.
Karna	Lady dear, I hear
	your words as in a dream. Look, the dark
	has deepened all around us. Now the spark

of all is out. The Ganga makes no sound.
To some forgotten home, illusion's ground,
you have led me, in the earliest morning
of awareness! Like an old truth dawning,
your words touch me with a witching power.
My childhood that never came to flower,
the darkness of my mother's womb, are swirling
all about me now. Is it a whirling
dream, or truth? Come near, lady of love,
and on my face, upon my brow above
and chin below, let your right hand lie.
I have heard it whispered of that I
was cast off by my mother. It has seemed,
so many times at night when I have dreamed,
slowly she is coming to see me again;
I say to her, weeping in sorrow and pain,
"Mother, open your veil, show me your face!"
The image vanishes and leaves no trace,
ripping away a dream of driving need.
Has that dream-figure come tonight indeed,
as Mother of the Pandavas revealed,
beside the Ganga, on the battlefield!
See, dear lady, over across the river,
in the Pandava camp the lamp-flames shiver;
this side, hear the mighty sound that's coming
from the Kaurava stables: hooves are drumming
of a *lakh* of horse. In the morning's light
the terrible battle will begin. Tonight
why did I hear, in Arjun's mother's voice,
the loving tones to make my heart rejoice
of my own mother? Why so singing-sweet

	upon her tongue does my name sound? To greet
	the Pandava five my heart flies out, a brother!
Kunti	Then come my child, come now with your mother.
Karna	Yes – I shall go – asking, doubting naught.
	I shall go without a second thought.
	Lady, you are my mother. It is all.
	My deepest soul is woken by your call.
	To victory-conch and the trumpet-of-war
	my ears are deaf. All I knew before
	of gain and loss is nothing now to me.
	A hero's fame, a battle's enmity,
	defeat and triumph – all these seem a lie.
	Take me where I am to go.
Kunti	Nearby
	to where the lamp-flames in the still camp gleam,
	to the pale sandy shore across the stream.
Karna	There a motherless one will soon be given
	a mother for ever. There, in the dark heaven,
	all night the North Star shines out in the skies,
	in your beautiful and generous eyes!
	Lady, say once more, I am your son.
Kunti	My son!
Karna	O why then, far from everyone,
	in the unknown blind world, a thing of shame,
	without the privilege of a family name,
	untended by a mother's eye – then why
	did you abandon me? To be swept by
	upon a current of scorn – to be exiled
	from all – a motherless, a brotherless child!
	Because we were held separate from each other,
	Arjun and I, we have been drawn together

since childhood, by an irresistible force,
a hidden blind tugging, holding to a course
of jealousy! Mother – are you all
without reply? Reaching through night's shawl,
your shame now touches my skin silently,
to close my eyes – so let it be, let be.
Why you abandoned me, cast me adrift
do not explain. The first earthly gift
of God, a mother's love, you stole away
from your own child – but now do not say
why those heavenly riches were denied.
Today you come to clasp me to your side –
explain this only.

Kunti   Into a hundred bits
struck by a hundred thunderbolts my heart splits
at your reproaches, child. It must be so.
But with five sons around me, do you know,
because of the curse of leaving you, my son,
with five sons near, in my heart there was none,
and in this world, ah, it has been for you
my arms are outstretched, searching? That one who
did not have a son's care, for him my soul
consumed by fire, burns fiercely – to extol
the god of the world with its flame-offering!
It has been a fortunate day, to bring
me to you. When no word could slip your tongue,
at that time I did a terrible wrong –
find a word now child to pardon me,
a guilty mother. Now more powerfully
than a word of censure will be heard,
let the flame of a forgiving word

burn away my sin, and as it sears
my heart, so it will make it clean.

Karna   My tears
are yours. Let me take the dust of your feet,
Mother, the dust of your feet!

Kunti   Not in the sweet
hope of holding you to my breast, my son,
have I come here to you. All that is won
at birth is yours. To give it back I came.
You have an inheritance to reclaim.
No charioteer's son – you are the son of a king!
My child, there shall be no more suffering
of insult. To five brothers be a brother.

Karna A charioteer's son – and Radha is my mother.
Nothing can afford me greater pride.
Let the Pandavas be on one side;
the other, Kauravas. I envy none.

Kunti Take back your kingdom by your might, my son.
By Yudhisthira with a white fan fanned,
with Bhim to hold your parasol in his hand,
your chariot by the hero Arjun driven,
and Dhaumya singing Vedic songs of heaven,
in triumph and in fame that never ends,
on jewelled throne, and in the midst of friends,
you will rule an undivided land.

Karna The throne! Can it come to me from that hand?
The offer of a kingdom do not make
to one who turns away and must forsake
a mother's offered love. I know not how
one can defraud and then again endow.
A mother, and the birthright of a king,

and brothers – you laid waste to everything
in an instant, as my life began.
Deceive my mother? Do you think I can?
If the charioteer's wife I betray
to find a royal mother now today,
if I break my bond with Duryodhan,
the Kaurava prince, and rush off to a throne –
then shame upon me!

Kunti   My son, you are great,
a hero true! O Duty that is our Fate,
such a heavy punishment you bring!
Who knew, alas, the little helpless thing,
the child I left, would one day find such power
as to return with weapons, one dark hour!
That down a road of night he would come back
and with his own cruel hand the sons attack
of his own mother! What a curse is here!

Karna Mother, there is no need for you to fear.
I tell you this, the Pandavas will win.
On the dark slate of night I read it in
the constellations' letters – and I learn
which way the dreadful war is going to turn.
In this dead-still moment, from the sky
that never ends, a song is coming by
into my heart, a song of unsuccess,
of failed attempts, of deeds of lucklessness.
I see an empty quietness of loss.
Then do not call on me to go across
and leave the side on which defeat will fall.
Let the Pandavas be victors all,
be kings – but I will never leave the side

of no reward, of hope that is denied.
Mother, on my very night of birth
you left me on the surface of the Earth
without a name or home. Again depart
as you have done before, with hardened heart,
and leave me here once more to be the same,
defeated, without lustre, without fame.
Only, lady, still before you go,
yet a blessing here on me bestow –
that tempted with a kingdom, victory, fame,
I take with me in death a hero's name.

1900

One Village

There is a village where we both belong,
    and that we do is all of our delight.
They have a tree from which the *doël*'s song
    sings out, at which my heart is free and light.
Two lambs she has, her pets, that much enjoy
    to graze the grass about our banyan tree.
The fence about my field if they destroy,
    I take them up and hold them close to me.

    This village of ours is called Khanjana,
    this river of ours is called Anjana,
    I know that what I'm called is known to one and all,
    that girl of ours – why, she is Ranjana.

Their neighbourhood is near our neighbourhood,
    between the two there only lies a field.
Bees will often come out from their wood
    among our trees their honeycombs to build.
A hibiscus garland floats on down
    from their paved worship-place to where we are.
Flower-blossoms in their area grown
    brim in basketfuls at our bazaar.

    This village of ours is called Khanjana,
    this river of ours is called Anjana,
    I know that what I'm called is known to one and all,
    that girl of ours – why, she is Ranjana.

Down this village lane of ours you see
    the mango-trees fill up with mango-flowers.
As linseed grows in their locality
    a crop of hemp shows in this field of ours.
When above their roof the stars ascend,
    about mine is the race of the south breeze.
When on their wood the *Srabon* rains descend,
    in mine the blossom's on the *kadam*-trees.

    This village of ours is called Khanjana,
    this river of ours is called Anjana,
    I know that what I'm called is known to one and all,
    that girl of ours – why, she is Ranjana.

1900

Indifferent

Today I'll glide up to no-one, I'll rest on my oars.
My mind is set upon nothing. On that it will pause.
    I'll go here and there regardless of need or of cause.
I am not the slightest interested in the news
of this or that. All cheerfully I choose
    to drift on down, since nothing upward draws.

Whatever I get, I'll take it and not reject it –
which is not to say I'll scramble to collect it.
    If it wants to make off, I won't delay its exit.
I'll scold at none and none will I hear scold.
Whatever deep in my mind's cup has rolled,
    I'll let it lie in the lees there, disconnected.

In the heart's games so often mortally wounded,
so often the dance of the anklet-bells I have sounded.
    I have pled with many for mercy and have not found it.
I have beaten on door after door. Again and again
as I beaded my tears into a garland-chain,
    my heart has let its dye run about and around it.

I have fled the cares of the mind, it's a holiday,
in no time at all I have come to the house of play.
    My heart-crushing load now down at last I lay.
Returning my shackle in pieces to where I got it,
I'll forget what there is to forget, though I never forgot it.
    After so long I have lifted my head up today.

So many flowers of Spring! – I had not noticed.
The business of choosing took up all my interest.
    Like a bee, I collected – I wanted the sweetest,
nectar-obsessed. All blind to beauty's traces,
I trampled uncaringly upon their faces.
    Lost in a *bakul*-bed, my self was displaced.

I travelled far today – my mind on not much.
And that is why to the three worlds I am such
    as to be sought out. With desire's fierce clutch
I reached to none. All blooming on their stems
I left   and left hope's lofty stratagems.
    Now all are thronging close enough to touch!

1900

New Rains

Today my heart dances, it soars, it soaringly dances,
    like a peacock it prances:
like a peacock's tail-quills quivering
a thousand thrill-colours shivering –
    while my soul is fixed on the sky
    staring adoringly.
Today my heart dances, it soars, it soaringly dances.

Boom-booming clouds burstingly grumble and rumble,
    skies tremble and tumble.
Down-above rains rush showering:
paddy-shoots see-saw: a cowering
    dove sits shaking on the nest,
    frogs croak deep-thirstingly;
and boom-booming clouds burstingly grumble and rumble.

Glistening rain-cloud-*kajol* tinges my eyes,
    blue fringes my eyes.
To deep shade and grass tender
my joys kneel and surrender.
    My soul's delight is under *kadamba*-trees
    awake now, listening.
The glistening rain-cloud-*kajol* tinges my eyes.

Look, on the castle whose hair is unravelling, flying,
    all the hair-knot untying?

Look, the deep blue sari-cover
across her breast now is drawn over –
     as with lightning she plays in the air,
          a here-there, here-there travelling –
look, on the castle whose hair is unravelling, flying?

Look, who has settled there in her dark green now,
          on the bank to be seen now?
For whom does she search the sky in a dream,
as her pitcher drifts off downstream?
     In the new grass she carelessly nibbles
          the jasmine fresh-petalled there.
Look, who has settled there in her dark green now?

Who is that swinging up, swinging down now in the *bakul*-tree,
          on her own, all free?
Loose-flock *bakul*-flower rocks by
as her sari-sash flies high,
          her locks of hair streaming out
               and round the eyes flinging up –
who is that swinging up, swinging down now in the *bakul*-tree?

Who has found in the bank-covering *keya*-bloom
          her shining boat's mooring-room?
Picking at clusters of moss until
her sari's loose folds round and fill,
          she sings heart-stealing songs
               of rain-time, tear-discovering.
Who has moored her boat in the bank-covering *keya*-bloom?

Today my heart dances, it soars, it soaringly dances,
     like a peacock it prances.
Drenched the new leaves, and the thicket
juddering to the chirping cricket . . .
        breaking its banks the river advances
          by the village soft-roaringly.
Today my heart dances, it soars, it soaringly dances!

1900

Krishna-Kali

Krishna-kali is my name for her.
  The village people call her "black", I fear.
In the field one cloudy day I saw
  the eyes of a dark girl as of a deer.
No trace of any veil was there to see,
her plait swung down behind her back all free.
  Black? However black she may appear,
  I saw the girl's black eyes as of a deer.

With deep clouds the day was overcast;
  two dark-coloured cows there started lowing.
From her hut the dark girl hurried out,
  quick-footed, busy, anxious in her going.
As she listened to the clouds' dark cry,
her twin eyebrows seemed to strike the sky.
  Black? However black she may appear,
  I saw the girl's black eyes as of a deer.

Suddenly an east wind tore across:
  the paddy-field had waves across its face.
I was standing at the ridge alone;
  only she and I were in that place.
Did she look my way? No one will tell:
only I know, and she knows as well.
  Black? However black she may appear,
  I saw the girl's black eyes as of a deer.

This is how the clouds of black soot come,
     in the month of *Jyaishtha*, from the north-east.
This is how, upon the *tamal*-trees,
     in *Asharh* the black shadows come, soft-fleeced.
This is how, upon a *Srabon* night,
the heart can take a sudden deep delight.
     Black? However black she may appear,
     I saw the girl's black eyes as of a deer.

Krishna-kali is my name for her.
     Let others say the names they like to hear.
In the Maynapara field I saw
     the eyes of a dark girl as of a deer.
She had no time to think that I was there,
that she should hide her head. It was left bare.
     Black? However black she may appear,
     I saw the girl's black eyes as of a deer.

1900

The Guest

Love came and went, and left ajar the door.
    No second entrance.
Only one more arrival, one guest more
    to make acquaintance.
One day he'll come in and the lamp extinguish,
    carry me far
down the trackway of some wandering homeless
    planet and star.

Till then I'll sit alone, by open door,
    work in attendance,
and when the time comes for that one guest more,
    there'll be no hindrance.
One day all the worship-rites I'll finish –
    prepared at last,
I'll spread my arms and welcome home the homeless,
    in silence vast.

The one today who left an open door,
    still by the entrance
said, "Dry your eyes, for there is one guest more
    to gain admittance.
Finish the weaving, all your work accomplish,
    pluck out life's thorn,
and to your new home carry – you, the homeless –
    a wreath newborn."

1902

Alone

You're sleeping now. I'll tend to the lamp and stay
    at the door awake.
Your loving's over. All the love today
    is for your sake.
For my sake you need never dress up more.
    But I'll array
my heart with flowers for you in endless store,
    both night and day.

Past tiredness, pain, the day's work without end
    do your hands know.
Today I'll lift them from all that, and bend
    to them my brow.
Your faith's complete, your heart and soul are rendered –
    you take your way.
From now in tears my faith to you is tendered,
    my praise-notes play.

1902

Sea-Shore

On the sea-shore of the world
    children come to play.
Above, the never-ending sky
stands still as the world goes by;
water dances, foamlets fly
    on the deep blue all day.
Voices on the shore rise high –
    children come to play.

They build in sand, they play with shells,
    all in a fine array.
On the huge blue water floats
a flotilla of toy boats,
and small hands craft a leafy raft
    in mood of holiday.
On the sea-shore of the world
    children are at play.

They cannot swim, they cannot cast
    a net in the right way.
For pearls a diver plumbs the deeps;
rich cargo-boats a trader keeps;
these set out pebbles in small heaps,
    and all for the display.
They do not search for gems, nor cast
    a net in the right way.

The sea and sea-shore foam and laugh,
    they laugh and foam with spray.
The terrible waves in a great throng
to the children sing a song,
as a mother rocks her child along,
    its fears all to allay.
The sea plays with the children, as
    the tide laughs in, away.

On the sea-shore of the world
    children come to play.
A storm rushes about the sky,
a far boat sinks, the waves rise high –
death's messenger flies on and by –
    idly still they stay
on the sea-shore of the world,
    children at their great play.

1903

In New Dress

Did you come at that time to my court, was it you then arriving?
    Delighted you smiled, with flute-song beguiled,
it was a day to be wild, *Phalgun* in its splendour was raving –
dear, was it you at the dawn of that day who came roving,
    at the court of new youth then arriving?

You let me forget the tide of work that besieges.
    What play then was here – did time disappear? –
the blood-red lotus swung sheer in my heart to your surges,
my soul was charged by your glance, by its languorous searches,
    I forgot the work that besieges.

Alas, I know not when sleep to my eyes gave its pause.
    I awoke with the sky all in cloud, deep and high,
on a bed of crushed leaves there lay I, under a tree in repose.
As you and I gathered flowers, and let the hours pass,
    sleep to my eyes gave its pause.

The court of that time is dissolved in today's steady downpour.
    The way's bare of late, I've shut door and gate,
my heart is lonely, prostrate in the rain's great ardour.
Did you knock at the door, shall I welcome you with fervour
    in today's steady downpour?

Now you have come in an ash-smeared ascetic's likeness.
    With fixed, level gaze your fiery eyes blaze,
a stream of water plays from your locks' matted thickness.

You have brought from outside in with you the tempest's darkness
    in your ascetic's likeness.

Dire, speechless and poor, enter my broken dwelling,
    to you I bow. A fire's script on your brow,
with your iron staff now, your iron bangles clanging and dinging –
don't leave with nothing, take my every belonging,
    my guest, at my broken dwelling.

1904

Death's Tryst

Why do you speak so soft and low,
    dear one, death of mine?
Is it love's way, to journey slow,
    and with your eyes to pine?
As to the stem are tiredly stirred
    flowers in dusk's gloaming,
as the cows come home in a herd
    after a day's roaming,
so calm you come: and of your word
    no meaning I divine.
Your footfall is more soft than all,
    dear one, death of mine.

Will you approach like this, O thief,
    dear one, death of mine,
to bring sleep for the eyes' relief,
    then to the heart incline?
In the numb blood then will you creep
    and set it to your motion?
Will they sound the chorus of sleep,
    your anklets' soft commotion?
And will you win me to your keep,
    and your cold arms entwine?
Why you come and go I do not know,
    dear one, death of mine.

Is this consummation's way,
    dear one, death of mine?

No auspicious customs, say,
　　splendid trappings fine?
Your tawny matted locks awry,
　　won't they know a proud tying?
Won't the flag be hoisted high
　　of victory, all sides flying?
Won't the river-bank's red eye
　　open to your torch-shine?
Won't the ground shake all around,
　　dear one, death of mine?

As Shiva sets out for his wedding,
　　dear one, death of mine,
details under every heading
　　state a great design.
His bull is roaring all around,
　　his tiger-hide is flapping,
snakes about his locks are wound
　　hissing, rearing, snapping.
To a slapping sound his cheeks rebound,
　　while from his neck's line
a string-of-skulls bobs, as his flute sobs,
　　dear one, death of mine.

Hearing the burning-ground-folk's roar,
　　dear one, death of mine,
Gauri's a-quiver, her tears outpour
　　in happiness divine.
Her left eye trembles, her heart leaps,
　　all is incoherence,
her body is sinking in joy's deeps.

At the wild groom's appearance,
    her mother strikes her brow and weeps –
a welcoming malign.
Her father foresees the loss of all ease,
    dear one, death of mine.

Why do you come a-stealing, thief,
    dear one, death of mine?
Night steals to dawn, or tears of grief
    steal down in sad decline.
Celebrate all night long, and blow
    the victory-conch, withhold me
(taking me by the hand), and so
    in blood-red clothes enfold me.
Pay heed to none: I freely go,
    to you myself consign.
Yet take me away in a fitting way,
    dear one, death of mine.

If for the house my duties be,
    dear one, death of mine,
shatter the work, embolden me
    such labour to resign.
If all my dreams come true and I
    lie in my bed's keeping,
if swathed in languor's sheets I lie
    half-awake, half-sleeping,
then fill the conch with Ruin's sigh –
    I'll speed, at that sign,
fast and faster, lord and master,
    dear one, death of mine.

I will go where your boat is buoyed,
    dear one, death of mine,
where the wind blows from an endless void
    behind the dark's wake-line.
Though the thunderous clouds come near
    from north-east, my way heading,
though the lightning's snakes uprear
    in fire-flame, their hoods spreading,
I'll not return in a false fear . . .
    but silent on the brine
row in the reddening great sea's flow,
    dear one, death of mine.

1904

If No One Turns

If no one turns to your lonely call, go on alone.
Out alone, out alone, out alone, go on alone.
If (unfortunate one) none says a word
but timid faces all turn away, unheard
        then opening all
your heart, let your dear word flower, speak out alone.
If (unfortunate one) on your dark journey
there is none to meet you, but all turn back blindly –
        then with your feet
bloodied by thorns of the path, step on alone.
If (unfortunate one) none offers you light
in the night that great storms disturb, but doors are shut tight –
        then with lightning's barb
alight at your chest's very ribs, burn on alone.

1904

Mother

When did you appear today, from the heart of Bengal,
in undreamt-of loveliness, to be seen by all?
Mother, I gaze on and on, your beauty I behold,
your door opened, you came out into a hall of gold.
A scimitar gleams in your right hand, your left in calm you raise,
a tender smile in your two eyes, and your third eye ablaze.
What image do I look upon, what lineament untold?
Your door opened, you came out into a hall of gold.
As the thunder hides within your full free-flowing tresses,
your sash is dazzling in the sky that the sunlight dresses.
Mother, I gaze on and on, your beauty I behold,
your door opened, you came out into a hall of gold.
Unblessed I thought you were, when I cared not your face to see,
abandoned in a broken hut to endless misery.
That lightless smile – where is it gone? That mean apparel –
                                                where?
Today the radiance of those feet is borne upon the air.
What image do I look upon, what lineament untold?
Your door opened, you came out into a hall of gold.
In sorrow's dark now let delight flood Earth in every part –
your *fear not* rings out in the heart, O conqueror of the heart!
Mother, I gaze on and on, your beauty I behold,
your door opened, you came out into a hall of gold.

1904

Dayspring

Rudra, your terrible light appeared today,
        piercing the door;
an arrow of lightning hurtled into my chest,
        and dreams' net tore.
I was debating whether to rise or not,
and if blind dark had gone from the skies or not,
and whether I should open my eyes or not,
        sleep's dullness clearing.
Then it was, Shiva, that the note of your horn
        came to my hearing.
        Roaring its roaring
    through holes of burnt cloud
        in the bright sky pouring,
    it struck. The East woke,
        its blushes slow-soaring.

Great one, what are you wearing? A snake is hissing
        upon your brow.
Is this the dawn tune that the *rudra-veena*
        is playing now?
Where is the *kokil* singing its rapt song?
Where are the wild flowers in their forest-throng?
It is as if the dark night, after long,
        were splintered through.
Your sword has sliced the buffalo of darkness
        into two.
        Earth hears pain's scream.

Blood-red light is falling from the heavens
in endless stream.
Some, awake, lie trembling on and on;
some, fearful, dream.

Your nameless servants of the burning-ground
hunger in the long night.
Licking their dry lips they cry and moan,
on, on, before the light.
They are the guests our home is waiting for,
and now they dance their dance on the yard-floor.
Come householder and open wide the door,
don't hide away.
Bring what you have, give what you have – till there's
no debt to pay.
Let none sleep – for the goal
is to present the very heart
in pieces in an offering-bowl.
What idle spell has kept you true
to a false love, O needy soul?

On the path to dawn whose voice is ringing out:
"There is no fear, no fear –
for those who give their being without stint,
no loss, no loss to bear."
O Rudra, how shall I sing your song?
Lord quicken me till playing along
to the death-dance beat I can sound strong
the hand-drum of my heart.
A dish shall be my offering
of sorrow's pain and smart.

It is morning now morning.
Shiva laughs a loud laugh
to end dark with dawning.
What deep joy to be
awake without yawning!

Lord of life, when we surrender life,
we know you best.
Your trumpet we must hear, with all our fear
now set at rest.
How good it is that in sky's stormy din
Ruin with matted locks can spread and spin.
How good the morning has come riding in
on the lion of cloud!
The rite of union flames out in the thunder
scorching loud.
Dark hours retreat.
I shall gain you great wealth
in my wealth's defeat.
I shall make death immortal,
touching death to your feet.

1907

Song Offerings

8

Today I'll watch the paddy play
   hide-and-seek in shadow-light.
Who has floated in the blue sky
   a boat of cloud so white?
      Today wild-circling in the sky,
      its honey forgotten, a bee whirls by.
      Today by the river why should a crowd
       of *chokha-chokhi* birds alight?

Hey, I'm not going home today brother,
   brother, I'll stay outside!
Hey, let's break the sky open today
   and plunder it far and wide!
      As if with tide-foam leaping and straying
      on the breeze, and laughing, and never still staying –
      today all idle, with some flute-playing
       the time will pass till night.

1909

56

Down from the lion-seat throne
    your way you made –
and at the entrance to my lonely room
    you stood, Lord, and stayed.
        Alone in my own world
          a song I was singing,
      and as your hearing caught the melody
        your way you made –
    and at the entrance to my lonely room
      you stood, Lord, and stayed.

In your court are so many songs,
    so many fine minstrels –
today it was an unskilled song that drew
    your love's great accolade.
      For when to the universal melody
        was added a sad tune,
      then taking in your hands a crowning garland
        your way you made –
    and at the entrance to my lonely room
      you stood, Lord, and stayed.

1910

64

Discard your used strings one by one,
    and where the spaces are
tie up the new strings on the old *sitar*.
      A courtly gathering
      will soon sit listening
    in dusk to one for whom the time has come
    to play a farewell tune to day's bazaar.
      Tie up the new strings on the old *sitar*.

O my dear open your door to me
    upon the sky and night
and let the silence of the seven worlds
    at your house alight.
      Now let the ending of the song
      arrive that you have sung so long.
    And that this instrument is indeed your own,
    even let this from your knowing vanish far.
      Tie up the new strings on the old *sitar*.

1910

68

When I used to play with you
  who you were no one would know.
No fear or heart's dismay with you
  was mine in life's exuberant flow.
    To woods and fields all without end
    you called me, as my closest friend,
    and I laughed and ran my way with you
    dawn after dawn, so long ago.

Such songs you sang out clear and whole –
  whose meaning, dear one, none might chart.
Only with those songs sang my soul
  and danced my ever-exuberant heart.
    But what do I see now the play is done?
    A silent sky, hushed moon and sun,
    a universe poised still, apart,
      that at your feet keeps its eyes low.

1910

100

Monsoon weather now I see
 all around humanity.
In an angry muttering
 it has come here, cloaked and shrouded.
Rising in a sky dense-clouded,
 furious at heart it dances –
and a mass of cloud advances
 over-running its own bounds.
Clasped in a close union
 clouds fly on unfaltering.
Who can tell what drives them on?
 From that drift the thunder sounds.
Monsoon weather now I see
 all around humanity.

Into the far-distant regions
 cloud-accumulations go
in their companies and legions.
 What propels them they don't know,
nor when they dissolve and fall,
 as the *Srabon*-torrents come,
from a great hillside to the sea.
 Do they comprehend at all
what land that was? where it might be?
 How grand and splendid they become!

Yet it takes them unawares,
    the terrible life and death that is theirs.
Monsoon weather now I see
    all around humanity.

In that tumbling over there
    in the havoc of the north-east,
where a storm takes on its nature,
    what is whispered on the air?
What irrevocable future,
    in the deepening shadows pieced
on the horizon, in night-stillness
    carries its own speechless pain?
As it reaches to its fullness
    in the dark skies of the brain,
black imagination leads
    into what forthcoming deeds?
Monsoon weather now I see
    all around humanity.

1910

106

O my soul, awaken slowly
  in this holy pilgrims'-place,
where India's greatness reigns, before
  the ocean's space.
    I spread my arms here – I revere
      and worship God-in-Man:
      his praise repeat, to joy's fierce beat,
        with all the heart I can.
    These thought-clad mountains, this field-ground
      with river-rosary-garlands wound,
      here each day always with your gaze
        the pure Earth you embrace,
      where India's greatness reigns, before
        the ocean's space.

No one knows from where it flows
  or who set it in motion,
this wild flood-force of humanity's course,
  to mingle in mid-ocean.
    Here are Aryans and non-Aryans,
      Moguls, tribes-of-East,
    and Huns and Scythians, Pathans, Dravidians,
      all in a body pieced.
    Now the West has opened its door –
    and bringing gifts all through it they pour,

to give, to take, their mixed mixing make . . .
    their way they will not retrace,
where India's greatness reigns, before
    the ocean's space.

All in uproar, awash with war,
    and singing victory's song,
past desert-track, over mountain's back,
    they made their way along.
    And still all, all within me call,
        no one is ever far,
    and still my blood remembers the thud
        of the different sounds of war.
    O *rudra-veena* play play play –
        those distant in their scorn today,
    their own door breaking and their way making –
        come, join us in this race,
    where India's greatness reigns, before
        the ocean's space.

Of old upon the heart-strings rolled
    Om in its great sound
unending where the One in prayer
    rose ringing all around.
    Through trial of austere self-denial,
        as various gifts were laid
    in the fire of the One – division was undone
        and one great spirit made.
    With that endeavour, that prayer today,
    the door stands open where the holy flames play . . .

now let us here stand close and near
    with lowered face,
where India's greatness reigns, before
    the ocean's space.

In the holy fire-maze see now ablaze
    sorrow's blood-red flame.
As it burns in the heart, to bear it is our part –
    it is written beside our name.
        O my soul, bear your burden whole,
           the call of the One come to know,
        and your shame and fear will be conquered here,
           and your sense of injury go.
        After intolerable pain is borne –
        what a magnificent life will be born!
        The Mother wakes in her nest. Day breaks
           at the end of night's slow pace,
        where India's greatness reigns, before
           the ocean's space.

O come Aryans, come non-Aryans,
    Hindus, Muslims, all,
come all of you, you English too,
    come you of the Christian call.
        Come here Brahmin, but first determine
           to clean your mind and so
        hold the hand of all. Come you who fall,
           let the great insult go.
        Come come quickly where the Mother is crowned,
        in this pilgrims'-place where the pots are found

that are not yet full of the touched-by-all-
made-holy-water-of-grace,
where India's greatness reigns, before
the ocean's space.

1910

107

Among the meanest your feet go,
    where all the destitute are tossed,
        among the least, among the low,
           among the lost.
    To touch your feet, in my heart's love,
    I vow – but my heart does not move.
Where your feet, suffering insult, go,
    there my heart's reverence has not crossed,
        among the least, among the low,
           among the lost.

Pride is denied your to-and-fro
    in ragged clothes of cheapest cost,
        among the least, among the low,
           among the lost.
    Where wealth and dignity abound
    I hope your friendship will be found.
But friendless homes that friendship know –
    there, where my heart has not crossed –
        among the least, among the low,
           among the lost.

1910

108

O my unfortunate land, for all those you shame,
the insult you endure shall be the same.
    For all you betray,
      rights taking away,
distancing from your warmth, denying their claim,
the insult you endure shall be the same.

From human contact holding yourself apart,
you stand aloof from the Lord of the human heart.
    When in God's wild anger
      comes famine-hunger,
to eke out your food with all must be your aim.
The insult you endure shall be the same.

When you dismiss from your throne in bullying style,
you carelessly thrust your own power into exile.
    Ground under heel
      with those you must reel
in the dust, there is no other way but to feel the blame.
The insult you endure shall be the same.

If you fling one down, he will have you tied and bound.
If you keep one back, he will drag you along the ground.
    If you cover and cloak
      in ignorance dark –
he will hide your good, its terrible distance frame.
The insult you endure shall be the same.

Ten thousand years since the burden of scorn began.
Still you ignore the God that is God-in-Man.
>Can't you look down, see
>where in the dust He
came down – and the god of Untouchables became?
The insult you endure must be the same.

You can't see the messenger of death standing outside.
You can't see his curse etched in the nation's self-pride.
>If you still won't call
>from the heart to all,
but all-apart, knot yourself to your pride's name –
in death's ash then endure with all the same.

1910

141

All my body, all my mind
I would at a stroke relinquish –
this black shadow leave behind.
Let that fire its shape abolish,
in that ocean let it vanish,
at those feet O may it perish,
    this delusion blind –
    all my body, all my mind.

When I see it occupy
a space, O Lord, for shame I die.
This shadow-mark of deepest dark,
    O take, cast far behind –
    all my body, all my mind.

In the heart what screen can be?
One and in entirety
will you appear when once you clear
    this delusion blind –
    all my body, all my mind.

1910

151

I will give myself to the hands of love
  and I await its claim.
Later and later is the hour,
  I more and more to blame.
    To law's tight knots I have been led,
    to fixed decrees – and I have fled,
    content to undergo instead
      the punishment that came.
    I will give myself to the hands of love
    and I await its claim.

People's scorn, their mocking stare –
  it is all merited.
From the lowest depths I bear
  the shame heaped on my head.
    But now it is the end of day:
    the market fair is done; and they
    have in their anger gone away
      who came to call my name.
    I will give myself to the hands of love
    and I await its claim.

1910

Bud

Closed up is the lotus bud of light,
   by the darkling leaf of evening tended.
When the dusk has crossed the sea of night,
   of itself it opens, flowering splendid.
Alone the dark I follow on the way
of pilgrimage towards the dawn of day.
   On the horizon now my day is ended.

The morning's fragrance, soft and far and high,
   is wafted down at times, through darkness straying.
A song is sleeping all-still in the sky,
   its breath has sent the tiny star-lamps swaying.
The hope of night that is immense, profound,
the speech of night in meditation drowned,
   in the sky of my soul seek out their saying.

Where life's road will lead when day has died
   is lost in the wild deep of darkness falling.
Pointing to the way, all steady-eyed,
   fear not stars are in their silence calling.
Plucking the last flower of the tired day,
I am going to end my journey's way,
   to find the shore of a new life's befalling.

O my evening, all I had with me
   safe within your sari-hem is lying.
Neighbour of night, a band-of-friendship see
   on your tender wrist of my hand's tying.

What memories of joy, what dawn hopes thrill,
what songs of dark, sweet griefs, are with me still,
   even at the time of life's farewell and flying!

All that was mine, all that is over and done,
   falling behind as I go, itself so freeing,
the beckoning gems – heart's racking storms – all gone
   to the horizon like a shadow fleeing,
that wealth of life will not be cast away.
In dark of dust's dishonour though it stay,
   it finds the touch of the feet of the All-Being.

1914

The Conch

In the dust your conch was lying: how could I endure it?
Air and light were cut off, dying – I could not ignore it!
Let the flag of fighters fly, songs be sung out in full cry,
a line of marching men go by with steps direct and sure!
In the dust I saw it lie, that fearless conch-of-war.

To the prayer-room I had turned to offer pleasing flowers.
Heaven's peace I might have earned, after day's long hours.
All the aching in my heart, I imagined would depart,
and my dark-stained soul would start, I thought now, to be pure.
Then I saw lying down apart in dust, your conch-of war.

Where does my prayer-lamp throw its flame, at this late hour
                                        of the day?
Shall I plait red buds in war's acclaim? Alas for the fine white
                                        spray!
To all my struggling round and round I thought an answer
                                        had been found:
that sheltering in your safe surround I'd live debt-clear, secure.
Then at once I heard it sound, your silent conch-of-war.

Give me a touch of the magic stone with power youth to impart!
Let me hear the *Dipak-rag* in the tone of the visionary glad heart!
Let night's ribs split – see through the rift the whole sky an
                                        enlightened gift –
now from the dark-horizoned drift night's fears will wake no
                                        more.
Today with my two hands I'll lift your victory conch-of-war!

I know I know that sleep will go and vanish from my eyes.
Harsh arrows will rain down, I know, as if from *Srabon*'s skies.
Some will hurry to my side, some will weep and stay inside;
some by nightmares will be tried that shudder from sleep's store.
But this day with joyful pride shall hear your conch-of-war!

I looked to you for peace before – and only shame I found.
Make my body fit for war, in clothes of battle bound!
Let new onslaughts beat and press – I will stand firm nonetheless –
in my heart at your distress a victory-drum shall roar!
I'll give all – and repossess your fearless conch-of-war!

1914

Picture

Are you merely a picture – a canvas-tint?
  The nebulae far-high
    that crowd the nest of the sky,
      those voyagers of darkness, with the glint
of a traveller's-lamp to hand, that night and day
    continually explore,
      planets stars sun,
  are you not as real as they?
    Ah picture – are you merely that, no more?

Why, within this endless restlessness
    do you not stir?
  O my dear pathless one,
      accompany the wayfarer.
    Night and day
  within the inner hall
of quiet eternal – motionless
    why do you stay?
You are within all yet so far from all.
    This dust
  lifting her grey sari-hem
    runs here and there in the wind's quick gust.
She tires of widow's weeds, discarding them
  in *Baishakh* – to attire in ochre robe
    a hermit-lady, Earth-ground of the globe,
  and here and there about her body then
    leaf-shape decorations she will pen
      at dayspring union, as Spring comes to pass.

Even this dust is real alas.
This grass
absorbed beneath the world's feet – it can thrill
in every blade, and every blade is real therefore.
You are a picture, silent-still,
a picture, nothing more.

Once you walked this way with us –
to breathing's impetus
your lungs would rise and fall,
about your body life had made, complete
its own fresh tune, its own new beat,
all to the world's beat matched, and all
a singing, dancing festival –
today it is so long ago!
In this life here,
in this world that I know,
you were so true and clear!
With beauty's brush you drew
in the universe on every side
images before my seeing
of the elixir of being.
The world's true word that morning then by you
I knew personified.

Together as we took our way –
sealed off in night's overlay,
you stopped. And I
in despair and in delight
continue on by day, by night.
In dark and light upon the sea of sky

the high tide still returns, to ebb away;
down both sides of the way
a mob of flowers of countless shades
with soundless feet is pressing by;
the rampant river of life cascades,
jangles the bangles of death, rill beyond rill.
To the tune of the unknown I go
far off and further still,
in an intoxication with the road.
But where you suddenly slowed
and left the way – your journey stopped, just so.
This grass, this dust, those stars, that moon and sun –
hidden by all that store,
at the back of all, each one,
you stay a picture – merely that, no more.

What mad poet's conjecture
is this? You – a picture!
Not simply a picture, no.
Who says that motionless
you stay, merely a brushwork-show,
in a dumb distress?
I'll stake my life, if that delight had ever
come to a halt, this river
had lost its wave, its speed so swift;
this cloud-drift
had erased its golden manuscript . . .
if the shadow of your shining tresses
from the Earth were stripped,
the *madhabi*-grove's murmurous caresses
that play

in shadows, in the quick breeze, on the ground,
would be a dream some day, one day,
no more to be found.

Have I forgotten you? It is because
it is at life's root now that you are set.
Absentmindedly I go along –
and do I not forget
the flowers, the stars?
Yet they make the breathing of life sweet,
and fill with song
oblivion's emptiness. So from your seat
at the heart of my forgetfulness, you sway
my blood. And to forget
is no forgetting then. There to be seen
you may not be – and yet
it is between my eyes that you are set.
And so today
you are blue within the blue, green in the green.
My universe
has found its deepest union in you.
Without my knowing (no one ever knew) –
your melody plays in my singing verse.
For you have been
the poet within the poet, at the core:
no picture, not a picture, something more.

One morning you were mine. In darkness then
I lost the person who was there before.
Now in the pitch black I reach you again.
– No picture, not a picture. You are more.

1914

The Restless One

O mighty river,
unseen, entire and free,
your waters silently
roll on for ever.
At your terrible bodiless speed the void shudders and shakes.
Hit by the furious blow of this insubstantial flow,
mass on mass of foaming matter wakes.
Out of the flying dark a violent beam
of light skims up in a colourful stream.
In a whirlpool-eddy,
like bubbles in a giddy
spinning-about, in tiers on tiers –
suns moons so many stars.

O Terrible Lady, O Indifferent One,
this aimless going, this endless travelling-on –
it is your song,
your silent tune. So far, so long
the distance – still it calls back in reply.
O that is why
a desperate passionate love possesses you,
as ever homeless, you go whirling by –
to that mad rendezvous!
Your necklace spins and flings,
the star-gems scatter; your stormy loose hair flies
and the void darkens; and the lightning springs
in swinging ear-rings; a sari-sash swishes in surprise
through trembling grass, past restless leaves that throng

the woodland all along;
        while flowers float down, the pathways filling,
    jasmine *champa bakul parul* down-thrilling,
            from your salver of the seasons spilling.

On you dash, you dash, you dash,
        only this, as out of sight you flash –
            ever-advancing,
            no backward-glancing,
        discarding all you have, as you run on,
    collecting nothing, everything is gone –
            there is no fear,
                no sorrow's care,
                only a sheer
            delight of speed, as onward you career
    and spend without reserve your journey's fare.

In the instant of your full being nothing is yours –
            and that is why
        on and on your purity endures.
    As your foot touches it and passes by,
    the universe's dust can then forget
        its filth at every moment – death can be
        life in a brilliance of bursting-free.
            If you let
    yourself a weary instant pause, stand still –
        the universe will choke and over-fill
at once with mountainous chunks of matter. Blind and dumb,
    deaf, crippled, headless – an obstacle will come
        great-bodied, terrible, preventing all;
        atoms will congregate in their own weight,

unmoving aberrations, that so small
will pierce the deepest heart of all the sky
with the spear-point of impurity.

Restless nymph, O dancing-girl,
beauty unseen,
the eternal swirl
of a heavenly river of dance makes pure and clean,
in a bathing-of-death, the cosmic life and being.
The sky blooms blue, clear endless, in its freeing.

"You poet, the tinkling of the ornamental dress
the universe sports, stirs in you today,
its causeless ceaseless going of unseen feet.
I hear the foot-sound of your restlessness
within my veins, and your heart's tingling beat
that no one knows – the sea-waves dance and play
within your blood, the forest thrills today
within your blood . . . I have a word to say.
I have come here, age on age,
from this life's stage to that life's stage,
in a quiet of quiet descending,
from this form into that one my way wending –
and always when I came along,
night or morning, all I had I spent
in one gift and another, till all went,
in this song, in that song.

Now look, the current's roaring out –
the boat is shuddering about –
abandon on the bank the hoard and stack

of your belongings. Don't look back.
      The word before you,
            let it draw you
      into the might
            of the great stream, all out of sight
            of tumult far behind, into a night
                of unfathomable dark, to endless light."

1914

Geese in Flight

In dusk's red shimmer Jhilam's winding stream
turned to dark in the dark, as a curved sword can seem
to hide away inside
its scabbard. Night's high tide
after the ending of the ebb of day
floated in on a dark water-way
flowers of stars;
beneath a mountain's blackness deodars
in lines were ranged. Creation would speak, it seemed –
as if the words were dreamed
it could not utter clearly. The dark was broken
by a great murmur, a heap of sounds unspoken.

Suddenly I heard
a lightning-glow of sound. The dusk-instant whirred
with a rushing-by
from far off to far further, in the field of the sky.
O wild geese flying,
your storm-intoxicated wings the sky-way plying,
with a great sound of joy and of mirth-making,
raised waves as they went by of wonder's waking.
That loud wing-whirl,
like an importunate *apsara* girl,
broke the silence with its deep thought filled.
The hill-range thrilled
now all in darkness covered,
the trees in the deodar-forest shivered.

It seemed, this word of wings
brought for a second to the heart of things
static and still
a thrill,
speed's trembling charge.
To be a cloud of *Baishakh* drifting at large
the mountain longed; while the trees yearned towards
that trail of sound – to loosen all the cords
tying them to the ground, to open wing, to fly
past all directions to the shore of sky.
Waves of pain, intent on the all-far, wake –
dusk's dream they break –
O wandering wings!
In the heart of All a passionate true word rings,
"Not here, not here, elsewhere!"

O geese flying through air
tonight you have taken away the cover
around me, of the silent-still. Below it I discover
in sky in water in ground,
restless and roaming-free, the same wing-sound.
In the ground's sky
the wings of the blades of grass go beating by;
under the earth's dark, who knows where,
thousands of geese of seeds are skimming to air;
new shoots are seen, wings spread. Tonight I see
hill and tree,
this mountain-range, this forest, wings flexed, re-flexed,
steer from one island, one unknown, to the next.
The pulse of the wings of stars startles the night
with a thin cry of light.

Many and many a true word
 of humankind I heard
  flying an unseen way
   from the dim past to a new age and day
    far off, not yet in bloom. At heart I heard,
flying with many and many another bird,
  in day and night,
   this homeless bird rushing in dark and light –
    from what shore to what shore?
In space the universe's wings sound out and soar,
  this is the burden of the song they bear,
   "Not here, elsewhere, elsewhere, elsewhere!"

1915

Eternal-I

When there's no signal of my footsteps up and down the way,
when at the *ghat* my ferry-boat will no more leave or stay,
   all the buying-and-selling ended, dealings over, debts refunded,
all the coming-and-going at market over for the day –
     it may be then that you will not recall me.
     You will not gaze up at the stars and call me.

When the dust rests and settles on the *tambura*'s strings,
and up and over all the doors a thorny creeper springs,
   and the flower-garden's wearing deep grass of the forest's
                           sharing,
while at lake-side far and wide the moss collects and clings –
     it may be then that you will not recall me.
     You will not gaze up at the stars and call me.

Then from this stage the flute will pipe up, even as now it plays,
the day will pass by even as if a day of nowadays,
   and just as now the ferry's loaded, *ghat* to *ghat* it will be
                          crowded,
over the field the cowherd-boys will play, the cows will graze.
     It may be then that you will not recall me.
     You will not gaze up at the stars and call me.

That I am not there on that morning – who is it can know?
This I will join in every game – who says it is not so?
   There will be a new name found me, there will be new arms
                        around me,

this eternal-I of mine will always come and go.
  It may be then that you will not recall me.
    You will not gaze up at the stars and call me.

1918

Being Lost

My tiny daughter, hearing her small friends shout,
down the large staircase was slowly setting out,
shading her lamp with her sari, with beating heart
slow, slow in the dark – stop-start, stop-start.

Out on the terrace, under *Chaitra*'s starred night,
I raced downstairs as I heard her cry of fright.
"What's up, Bami?" As the stairs she down-crossed,
the lamp had gone out. She wept, "I am lost, I am lost!"

Back under the stars – I seemed to see in slow journey
a girl like my Bami, alone, and her blue-of-sky sari
shielding the light. If it blew out, wind-tossed,
the heavens would fill with the cry, "I am lost, I am lost!"

1918

Remembering

I don't remember Ma.
Except I'm playing sometimes and – aha,
a tune's about, I don't know how it came,
something of Ma is joining in my game.
She'd sing out as she rocked me, to-and-froing –
she's gone, and left a song back in her going.

I don't remember Ma.
Except at dawn when *siuli*'s petal-star
wafts its scent on *Ashwin*'s dew-wet air,
something of Ma comes drifting in – from where?
There was a time she carried trays of flowers,
and now the *puja*'s fragrances are hers.

I don't remember Ma.
Except when – sitting alone, I look out far
from a corner of the bedroom at the blue sky –
and her still gaze is on me, I don't know why.
She used to cherish me on her lap once.
Now all the sky still has her loving glance.

1921

Asharh

From across the ages *Asharh* steals into my heart and brain.
Who's the poet in whose numbers sounds the thrumming of
the rain?
Garlands of the loves of old, now mere dust in dust untold . . .
on the damp air drifts the fragrance of the living blooms again.

Such a mass of cloud lay by the Reba river long ago;
on the hilltops of dark green one day the rain fell even so.
Then at the road, her lover gone, the Malwa girl gazed on
and on . . .
that look of hers is drifting in today beneath the clouds' black
stain.

1922

The Game

Now at dusk, my playmate, what is this game
                    you call me to?
Why excite with a lamp of colourful flame
                    a barren view?
In what light have you sealed and hidden away
a whim of dawn within your breast all day,
to catch from lotus now a glimpse of a ray
                    for night's fresh hue?
Will dawn be sketched, in a gold of dying away,
                    in dusk's lamp too?

The flute I lost at hide-and-seek, as if
                    it stole away –
where did you find it, under what dry leaf
                    on woodland way?
The tune you taught me, sitting close to me
on dew-wet grass beside dawn's banyan-tree,
even now in sighs, in tears, all suddenly
                    I hear it play –
the note the wild wind used to breathe to me
                    on woodland way.

The playmate of my dawn with *champa*'s gold
                    would baskets fill.
And now in darkness – is it lost? – that old
                    scent comes to thrill.
In new dress, past the *bakul*-trees, steps springing,
did she call me to the game? With hair wild-swinging

is that her now – the tumbling *champas* bringing
  in the basket still?
From that strange land to this, new-lost, fresh-springing
  does that scent spill?

What do you ask of me, Leader-in-Play,
  what kind of sport?
As day began, shall the ending of day
  be of that sort?
I rose at dawn to a breaking-of-locks, a free going,
in a mad wind to a wild nowhere blowing.
Shall I join the madcaps, all work overthrowing –
  be driven distraught?
Shall I chase the deer of dreams, in a to-and-froing
  set all at nought?

Chained to the way, as I follow in work's strong stream,
  will you forestall me?
In the wood's darkness where the fireflies gleam,
  is it why you call me?
In the pull of the causeless making all cares depart,
yet waking a strange quick anguish in the heart,
where do you wait, with a song to shiver and start
  in the air to recall me?
Knowing no way, swift to your breast I shall dart,
  it is why you call me.

You want no ritual garland, playmate dear,
  I know, I know.
A lamp of fragrance lights the bare ground here,
  no sacred glow.

Your play and my play shall be one, to sport
at the stars' carnival, the night's hushed court . . .
till with your *veena*, my flute in consort,
      the night will flow.
The game goes on, my light by your light caught,
      no sacred glow.

1924

Hope

For long I was yearning –
    a quiet spot to find
    for freedom of mind;
not honour, not riches, but to my own small home
        my thoughts ever turning.
To the trees' tender shade, the river's flow,
to the dusk's stars as all things homeward go;
above the water to dawn-light's descent.
outside the window to the jasmine's scent.
    The time's swift hour
    with this shall flower,
a smile, a tear of life ever returning.
Not honour, not riches, but to my own small home
        my thoughts ever turning –
            it was my heart's yearning.

For long I was yearning –
    to let range whole
    my thought-filled soul;
not honour, not riches, but to my own true word
        my thoughts ever turning.
In cloud the setting sun dabs its down-going
with the last colours of the fancy's knowing;
with light, shade, movement, magic in my hue,
my own kingdom of dreams I will build too.
    The time's swift hour
    with this shall flower,
a smile, a tear of life ever returning.

Not honour, not riches, but to my soul's true word
    my thoughts ever turning –
       it was my heart's yearning.

For long I was yearning –
    a deep thirst to slake
    and heart's nectar take;
not honour, not riches, but to a little love
    my thoughts ever turning.
To say a dear name with a song in the saying,
with no cause to be close, hand to hand straying;
to be far off, out with one's thoughts, past reach,
and again near, eyes glowing and brimming with speech.
    The time's swift hour
    with this shall flower,
a smile, a tear of life ever returning.
Not honour, not riches, but to a little love
    my thoughts ever turning –
       it was my heart's yearning.

1924

My Last Spring

Before day's hours depart,
and a new time's to start,
we'll gather and bring all the flowers of Spring –
this is the wish of my heart.

　Often will your garden see
　the month of *Phalgun* – let a *Phalgun* be
　this once, so may I ask, for me.

All unaware was I
as time slipped idly by;
now dusk comes on, my time is gone,
I see it in your eye.

　Like a miser I count out
　the minutes of my Spring. I go about
　in hesitation and in doubt.

Fear not: in the Spring bower
of your garden's flower
I'll not delay, nor seek to stay
at the farewell hour.

　I will not look back at you
　to catch a tear, forever to soak through
　the memory, a sweet-sad dew.

Listen, don't go away,
it's not the end of day.
There's time awhile, so time to beguile,
allow no thought to stay.

From behind a leafy screen
the afternoon's small light comes. Let its sheen
for now on your dark hair be seen.

Reckless, unreasoning quite,
laugh your laugh of delight.
At lake-side scare the squirrels there
into a sudden fright.

Words of old, words past recall,
I shall not remember them at all,
at which your restless step might stall.

You'll go. Your light step will sound
crackling dry-leaf on the ground.
A nest-returned rabble of birds all will gabble
into the twilight around.

Into the evening's darkening shade
of a thicket of bamboo, your form will fade.
The last flute-note of dusk is played.

When night is dark, my sweet,
sit at your window-seat.
The path will wind, I'll leave all behind –
and we no more shall meet.

Then cast it out of view,
a wan wreath, *mallika*-spun when light was new.
Your touch it will be, your adieu.

1924

The Tie of The Road

The road has tied a knot that does not bind us,
and we two travel with the wind behind us.
    An imp of dust, quick as a tick,
    sparkles the soul with a powdery flick.
    A goddess dances the Dance of the Ways
        in a cloud, robe-shimmering . . .
    at once the heart is softly ablaze,
        aglow and glimmering.

We do not have a golden *champa*-bower,
or woodland paths strewn with the *bakul*-flower.
    But suddenly in twilight dusk
    a nameless flower breathes out its musk.
    And in the morning from high branches,
        with a withering scorn,
    rhododendrons in their bunches
        mock the rays of dawn.

No wealth is ours, amassed in rich collection,
no home is ours, affording safe protection.
    A bird tail-dances by the way,
    we will not cage it, shut it away —
    we both delight in its wing-opening,
        its freedom-fortunate song.
    A rare and unexpected happening
        lights the way along.

1928

Unafraid

We two will not trace Heaven's art
    on Earth in wondrous tear-filled songs;
nor celebrate our wedding-night
with a sweetness sad and bright
    that to Cupid's darts belongs.
We are no suppliants at Fate's foot
    to beg a blessing with faint soul.
Nothing's to fear, we know it, dear –
    you are, I am: that is the whole.

We'll fly the flag of love high up
    a rocky path, with rushing speed,
submit to every task – and when
a grief is ours, accept – for then
    for peace or solace where's the need?
If the sail's rope rips and the rudder snaps,
    the river's waters round us roll,
we'll know, in Death's face standing so –
    you are, I am: that is the whole.

We have seen the all in each other's eyes,
    we have seen each other too.
Upon the desert's burning way
no mirage led our minds astray,
    no lie did we pursue.
While we two live, to walk with pride
    on Earth, shall be our role.

My love, a great word now is heard.
  You are, I am, it is the sum,
    it is the sum and whole.

1928

Cornet

Milkman Kinu's lane.
A two-storey building,
a ground-floor room with iron bars
right on the street.
Here and there the mortar's come away
from the mouldering walls, damp stains here and there.
A picture of Ganesh the God of Success
fixed over the door,
printed on cheap cloth.
Besides myself
the room has another inhabitant
at no extra rent –
a gecko.
It differs from me only in this,
it has enough food.

Junior clerk in a mercantile office –
a pay-packet of 25 rupees.
Only by teaching the boy at the Dattas' place
can I earn enough to eat.
I go to Sealdah Station,
spend the evening there,
it saves the cost of a light burning.
Whooshing engine-steam,
shrilling whistles,
swarming passengers,
yells of "Coolie!"

10.30 p.m. comes round
and I go back to my room, the silent lonely dark.

My paternal aunt's village on the Dhaleshwari –
her husband's younger brother has a daughter
who was betrothed to a certain poor wretch.
An auspicious time was set – and so it proved –
I fled that very moment!
At least the girl was saved.
I was as before.
She didn't come to my home, but she is never far from my mind –
in a Dhaka sari, *sindoor* on her brow.

It's been raining non-stop.
I'll have to shell out more on tram-fares,
they keep docking my pay.
Here and there in the lane,
heaps of rot –
mango-skins, mango-stones, jackfruit-pith,
fish-gills,
dead kittens –
refuse, God knows what.
The state of my umbrella
is that of a pay-packet that's been leaking fines –
it's riddled with holes.
The office uniform
is like Gopikanta Goshai's unctuous mind –
invariably sopping wet.
The dark shadow of the rain
lies in my damp room

like a trapped animal,
        paralysed, comatose.
            Day and night it seems to me
                I'm bound hand and foot to a half-dead world.

Kantobabu's at the top of the lane –
    long hair finely combed out,
        rather large eyes,
            the delicate taste of a dandy.
        His hobby's the cornet.
            At times one hears a tune
    on the lane's sordid air –
    sometimes at dead of night,
        or in the half-light of dawn,
    sometimes in the afternoon
        in a glitter of light and shade.
            Suddenly at dusk
                the *Sindhu-Baroyan* plays out –
    eternal Time's deep pain of separation
                sounds all over the sky.
            In a trice I know it –
                this lane is a great lie,
        the ravings of an insufferable drunkard.
            And suddenly I see
    between Emperor Akbar and Haripada the clerk
        there's not a whit of difference.
            In a cornet's plaintive appeal
                a torn umbrella and an imperial parasol
                    have gone off as one, to the same heaven.

Where the melody is true
   in an auspicious never-ending dusk
     there
         the Dhaleshwari flows,
  its banks all in the shade of *tamal*-trees –
    where in a yard
    someone is waiting
  in a Dhaka sari, *sindoor* on her brow.

1932

Ordinary Girl

I'm an inner-room girl,
        you won't know me.
    I've read your last book of stories, Sarat-babu,
        A Garland of Withered Flowers.
Your heroine Elokeshi was in a life-crisis –
        at the age of thirty-five
she was locked in combat with the age of twenty-five.
    I knew you were noble of heart
        when you allowed her to win through.

      To tell my own story –
        I'm young;
      and when a certain person was attracted
    by the magic sheen of my soft youth,
my body knew it and was in ecstasy.
    I forgot that I'm such an ordinary girl,
        with thousands of other girls just like me,
          the spell of innocence on their youth.

    I beg you,
please write the story of an ordinary girl.
    She's suffered a lot.
If there is something remarkable
      somewhere lodged in the depths of her nature,
      how will she show it?
    How many can find what's special in them?
When their eyes are filmy with soft youth

they're not about to seek out reality –
we are sold for the price of a mirage.

To say why all this arose –
let's call him Naresh.
He told me, no one had dazzled his eyes like me.
Such big words, I don't dare to trust them –
but it's so hard not to listen!

One day he went to England.
He sent the occasional letter.
In my heart I shuddered, oh God, so many girls are there,
such a jostling crowd of them!
And no doubt each one's special –
intelligent and beautiful!
And maybe they've all lit on one Naresh Sen,
whose unique quality lay undiscovered in his own land.

In the last post, he wrote in a letter,
Lizzie and he went to bathe in the sea.
(He quoted a passage from a Bengali poem,
those lines where Urvashi rises from the waves.)
And then that they sat side by side on the sand –
in front of them the blue waves are rolling
and sunshine's spread throughout the heavens.
And then, that Lizzie breathed gently at him,
"One day you arrived, the next you're off –
our two halves of an oyster-shell,
let them be filled at the centre
with a frozen tear-drop,
priceless and rare."

A most impressive turn of phrase!
And then our Naresh adds,
"If it sounds artificial, what's wrong with that,
            the words are beautiful –
to set gold flowers with diamonds – is it true or false?"
            You can understand
I felt a hint of comparison in this letter
      that pierced my heart like an unseen thorn –
         I'm a very ordinary girl.
   To pay full cost for a precious object,
            do I have the treasure to hand?
   Very well then, let it be –
            I'll stay in debt my whole life.

At your feet I beg, write a story, Sarat-babu –
      the tale of a most ordinary girl –
an ill-starred one from afar who must vie with
   at least half-a-dozen extraordinary beings –
            a "seven-woman-warrior" attack!
   I see that my fortune's a shattered one,
            I've lost the game.
   But please, the girl you write of,
         let her win through for my sake –
            let the reader's heart swell with pride!
   Let your pen's imprint be laurelled in honour.

         Name your heroine Malati.
            That's my name.
      There's no fear of its being found out,
   there are any number of Malatis in Bengal,
      and all are ordinary girls –

they don't know French or German,
they know how to cry.

How will you make her triumph?
Your mind is lofty, your writing noble.
Perhaps you will take her along the path of sacrifice
in exquisite suffering, like Shakuntala.
Take pity on me.
Please come down to my level.
As I toss and turn in bed in night's darkness
I ask God for the impossible,
for a boon that cannot be mine,
and yet it may be allowed to your heroine.
Why don't you put Naresh in London for seven years
repeatedly failing his examination?
Let him bask in the admiration of his bevy of female
worshippers!
In the meantime let Malati pass her M.A.
from Calcutta University,
by a stroke of your pen standing first in Mathematics.
But if you stop at that point,
your position at literature's pinnacle may be a little clouded.
Let my condition rise to what it will –
don't peg down your imagination –
you are no miser like the god who rules our fates.
Send the girl to Europe.
The wise people there, the learned, the valiant there,
the poets and artists and kings,
let them come flocking to her from all directions.
Let them discover her as astronomers may a new star –
not only as a learned woman, but as a woman;

let the world-captivating spell of her
work its power – not in a witless land,
    but where there are discerning minds, great hearts –
    the English, the Germans, the French.
Let an assembly be called in honour of Malati,
an assembly of very big names.
Imagine, there is a perfect storm of flattering words,
    in the midst of which she is walking casually,
    like a sailing-boat over waves.
       They see her eyes and all are whispering –
they say, India's moist clouds and burning sunlight
have met in that bewitching glance.
    (Here I will say in private,
the Creator did indeed bestow a special favour on my eyes –
    I have to say this for myself,
    for to date it has not been my fortune to meet
    a European to appreciate them.)
And let Naresh be there standing in a corner
with his bevy of oh-so-extraordinary girls.

    And after that?
    After that,
my potato-patch is cleared and my dream's disappeared.
    Alas for the ordinary girl,
      alas for the Creator's wasted wealth!

1932

Path

An endless path to your gate was the path I found:
  from the desert's rim to Nature's fresh green it wound.
I took up wet *juthi*-blossoms from the path's floor,
  my tender love in fragrant garlands to pour —
    don't shame it, spurn it, ignore!
The rain-cloud's shadow deepens in the trees,
  the pain of missing the path is heard on the breeze.
I saw from far your window-lamp burn quiet —
  with the eyes of a desperate bird in storm's dark riot.

1935

Earth

Today accept my salutation, Earth,
    as I make my final bow at the altar of day's end.

All-spirited one, the prize of heroes,
    tender and cruel are face-to-face in you,
        you are composed of woman and of man,
you dandle human life in a dour conflict.
    Your right hand pours nectar's tint without stint,
        your left hand splinters the bowl.
The field of your loving play you fill with a scornful echo.
You agonise the hero's life that aspires to greatness.
    You set an all-high price on the good. The pitiable one you
                                        do not pity.
In your trees and plants you hide the war of the moment,
    in fruit and crop they wear a victory-garland.
On land and water, in your pitiless arena of battle,
in the face of death, is the triumphant victory-shout of life.
        On the foundation of your ruthlessness
civilisation's victory-gate is set. At each error the full price:
                        destruction.

In your history's dawn the savage's might was dominant:
        he was barbaric, he was ignorant. he was harsh.
    His fingers were coarse, little used to skill and craft;
mace and club in hand, he would ransack stream and mountain;
    with fire and smoke he made the sky a nightmare.
        In the inanimate realm he was king,

and of all living he had a blind envy.
God came in a later age, read the mantras, the savage subsided –
an insensate arrogance was overcome.
The mother of life sat with a green sheet outspread.
Dawn stood on the summit of the eastern hill;
on the shore of the west the dusk descended, the urn of peace
balanced on her head.

The savage was fettered, gentled,
but the primitive barbarian has clung to your history.
In a moment he creates chaos –
out of the black burrow of your instinct
in a trice he wriggles free.
His madness is dormant in your veins.
God's mantra wells up in sky and breeze and forest
murmuring day and night notes high and low.
Still from the underworld of your heart the half-tamed
serpent-demon
rears its hood now and then –
under its scourge you assault your own Life,
devastate your own Creation.

Today with my life that is ravaged and marked with scars
I shall place an offering at your altar that is built of good
and evil,
and bow to your terrible beautiful grandeur, and depart.
The blind widening and awakening of vast Life and Death
that is under your ground, today I touch it, I sense it with
body and mind.
Countless extinct bodies of humans of countless ages are
gathered in the dust.

Among the name-devouring form-devouring
identity-devouring silent sands,
as the final fruit of all my sorrow and joy
I shall leave behind a few handfuls of dust.

Earth locked in a fixed restraint, Earth lost in a panoply of clouds,
in meditation imbued in a grand reticence of mountain-peaks
in rows,
Earth loud with the clamorous song of the ever-wakeful waves
of blue waters,
you are lovely in the wealth of your crops and in their dearth
cruel.
Here in your crop-field bowed with the ripening paddy
the clear sun of dawn each day wipes away dewdrops
softly brushing the scarf of its rays;
in the swinging uproar of green shoots the setting sun leaves
an unspoken message,
"I am glad."
There in your desert field pale with fear, starved of water
and fruit,
is a ghostly dance of a mirage among skeletons.

In *Baishakh* I've seen your tempest arrive like a black vulture
to snatch away a horizon already beak-stabbed by lightning.
All the sky roars like a lion with bristling mane;
it lashes its tail and a crestfallen tree crashes
prone in the dust with pell-mell branches.
Broken roof-thatch flies up in the wind's rising
like a jailed dacoit flinging off shackles.

Again in *Phalgun* I've watched your warm south wind scatter
the intimate ravings of love's union and parting in the fragrance
of mango-blossom.
Over the lip of the moon's cup spills the froth of heavenly wine;
in the impudence of the breeze the soft forest murmur
loses its composure to erupt in a wild chatter.

Gentle you are, cruel you are, old woman, young woman ever
you are;
from the sacrificial fire of Creation you came
with no beginning, in a dawn past distance of number;
you have cast down the ways of your pilgrimage's wheel
the relics – now meaningless – of broken histories;
unfeelingly you strew your rejected creations
here and there in the uncountable strata of oblivion.

Foster-mother of the living, you have reared us in the tiny cages
of your fragments of time;
in these all games have an end, each deed has its closure.
Today I stand before you in no false hope:
the garland of days and nights I have woven so long,
for this I claim no immortality at your door.
The vast moments that constantly open and close
on the path of your revolution round the sun over billions
of years,
if I have informed a trifling fraction of these
with the true worth of a visitor's role,
if I have attained to a fruitful phase of life
out of a deep sorrow,

then daub my forehead with a victory-sign of your clay.
That sign will fade away
in the night in which all signs dissolve in the final unknown.

Indifferent Earth,
before you altogether forget me,
today at the edge of your merciless feet
I offer my salutation.

1935

Flute-Player

"O flute-player
play your flute,
and let me hear my new name" –
I said it in the first letter I wrote,
do you remember?

I'm a girl of your Bengal.
When he made me, the Creator
didn't take the time to make a whole person,
he left the job half done.
The outside and inside have not joined as one,
the then and now of me –
my hurt is all at odds with my wits,
my strength to act not in touch with my strength of longing.
He did not set me in the boat of the age that crosses the river.
I was left on the other side of the current of Time,
high and dry on a sandbank.
From it I see
in a haze of bright lights, a faraway world.
For no reason a beggarly mind is beside itself –
I spread out my arms,
they find nothing to touch in any direction.

Time stands still.
I sit and look at the high tide's water.
To freedom's shore the ferry is floating by,
Dhanapati's boat is floating by,
the brief hour's light and shade is floating by.

And then your flute sounds out
with a song of life at the full –
to the pulse of the dead day
a vital speed returns with a thunderous beat.

What is it you are playing?
What pain awakes – and who is it who feels it?
Maybe it is a boat-song, set in the dominant,
of the fresh youth of the south wind.
– I am listening to the story of myself,
a babbling streamlet at the mountain's foot
in whose heart, all at once, *Srabon*'s night of rain
released its storm.
In the morning, what is this, the banks are washed away –
the spinning vortex of the intolerable current
is digging and dragging at the stubborn stones.

The notes you play fill my bloodstream
with the call of the storm, the call of the flood,
the call of the fire,
and crashing at the ribs, death's ocean-call –
a door-chain-rattling call of a careless wind.
As if the thieving gang of a full current
came roaring into a narrow gorge
of unfulfilment –
so to rip me away, set me adrift.
A frenzy of trees in a summer-storm cyclone
rants and raves in my limbs.

God gave me no wings to fly –
but he gave your song to my dream,

a winged soul's madness in a stormy sky.

At home I do my work quietly,
all commend me.
They see no violent desire,
no hubbub of greed –
if my head reels from misfortune's blow,
I lower my head to the dust.
I don't have the courage to give him a sharp knock,
the one who says No, that sentry, to thrust him
aside –
nor do I know how to love strongly,
only to weep,
to wilt at someone's foot.

Flute-player
your flute sounds out,
I am called to somewhere immortal.
There in its true importance
my head holds itself upright.
There my life is a sun new-risen
that has torn mist's curtain away.
There my eagerness that brooks no bounds
opens its wings of fire
out upon the unknown way of the sky –
a Gorur instinct with a ravening hunger.
She wakes, the rebel-woman,
with a burning sidelong glance conveys her hatred –
for the crowd of faint-hearts all around,
for the cowardice of narrow twisted minds.

Flute-player
maybe you have wanted to see me.
Where it should be I don't know,
when it should be I don't know,
or how you will know me.
That woman now, on a path that escapes being seen,
has taken herself to a love-tryst with you,
in shadowy form, in a night of *Asharh*,
with no one else there but the crickets chirping.
On that unknown form
in so many springtimes you have set a garland of tunes –
the flowers will not wither.

Hearing your call one day
a timorous girl who stays at home
has come out from a dark corner,
a woman who has cast her veil away.
She is like a sudden new song made by Valmiki,
amazing even you.
She will not come down from her seat of song;
staying in the half-light of a melody,
she will write letters to you,
you will not know her whereabouts.
O flute-player
let her stay there, at a flute-tune's distance.

1936

Africa

In that original pell-mell age
    when the Creator continually vexed with himself
overthrew his new creations again and again,
    while often he shook his head in those days with impatience,
        from the breast of the Earth of the East
  the savage arms of the ocean
carried you off in plunder, Africa –
enclosed you in the close guardianship of forest-trees,
    in the uncharitable light of a withdrawn room.
There at your lonely leisure
    you gathered secrets of a blind going;
    identified strange signals of water, land and sky;
    the viewless magic of Nature
awoke a hymn in the dark deeps of your mind.
    In the disguise of ugliness
    you taunted the terrible one;
        in the urge to stamp out fear
you made yourself wild in a terrifying splendour
  with the sky-rending drum of a dance of destruction.

  O shadow-hidden,
    under a dark veil
your human face was unknown
    to the tainted vision of disregard.
    They came with iron handcuffs,
they came with nails sharper than those of your wild wolves,
    the band of man-catchers
in a pride blinder than your unlit forest.

The savage greed of civilisation
unmasked its shameless inhumanity.
With your wordless weeping on misty forest-paths
the dust turned to mud, mixed with your blood and tears,
under the spiked boots of pirate-feet
a ghastly lump of clay
left a permanent mark on your insulted history.

Even then over the sea in village and town
bells of worship were ringing in churches
early and late in the name of the mercy of the Lord;
children were playing in their mothers' laps;
the song of the poet struck up
the welcoming ceremony of beauty.

Today when on the Western horizon
a stormy wind is suffocating day's end,
when animals have emerged from their hidden caves –
and inauspicious trumpet-sounds have told the death of day,

Come, poet of the time's turning
as evening deepens, in the last sunbeam
approach the doorway of a ravaged woman,
to say "Forgive me" –
so in its malevolent delirium
this may be the final gospel of your civilisation.

1937

Signs

Over the tracks of the vagrant breeze
    blossoms drift;
at your feet I have gathered these –
    take take my gift
with tender hands; and when I leave,
    with a sweet pain
remember me; for as your fingers weave,
    they'll bloom again.

That sleepless one, the *boukathako* bird
    in vain gives voice.
There are two whose every whispering word
    and consummate joys
by a full stream of light are swept away
    in *holi*'s moon.
These signs you'll thread to garlands the next day
    at lazy noon.

1939

Impossible

I thought the gulf between us was unbridgeable,
and went about alone, I knew not where.
Above the tree-tops *Srabon*'s cloud swoops blackening,
the lightning splits the heart of the night-air,
far off I hear the Baruni's torrent quickening –
and the mind says *Impossible, no, impossible!*

On such a night so often she'd lie comfortable,
head on my arm, hearing my verses' song –
the forest thrills to the thrumming of the downpour,
in body and mind she's one, for whom I long –
and now it's back, that night of *Srabon*'s splendour –
and the mind says *Impossible, no, impossible!*

I go out into night's depths. Nothing is visible,
a sky-song sings in the blood in the streaming rain;
juthi-scent sweetens the breeze; an intimation
from a wreath on her plaited hair, that I would gain,
from the new *malati* sends its inspiration –
and the mind says *Impossible, no, impossible!*

Though I am lost and in my going insensible,
how often that window has lit the way for me!
The *sitar* let me hear a certain tenor;
I knew my tear-entangled melody.
You left the bard and gave him a bard's honour –
and the mind says *Impossible, no, impossible!*

1940

186

Open the Door

Open the door,
liberate the blue sky;
let the inquisitive flower-scents enter my room;
the light of the early sun,
let it flood my body from vein to vein;
I am alive, the word of greeting that's throbbing
in every twig and leaf, let me hear it;
this dayspring dawn,
let it swathe my heart and mind with its scarf as it does the field
green with the shoots of new grass.
The love I have known in my life
utters its silent language
in the sky, in the air, everywhere.
I am bathed in the light of its pure enthronement.
All that's real I see as a necklace of jewels
on the breast of the blue.

1940

In the Dim Twilight

In the dim twilight all of a sudden I saw
Death's right arm locked round Life's neck, knit there
  in a tissue of red threads.
    I recognised the two at once.
  I saw Death's wife take her dowry
    as the groom's greatest gift.
With her on his arm he moved to the end of an era.

1940

On the Bank of the Rup-Narayan

On the bank of the Rup-Narayan
    I awoke.
I knew the world
      to be no dream.

In letters of blood
    I saw the shape of my being –
in hurt on hurt,
    blow after blow
      I knew myself.

Truth is cruel.
    I loved the Cruel One –
      He never defrauds.

A penance of grief till dying
    is life. To attain the terrible value of truth.
      To pay back the last coin of debt in death.

1941

The Sun of the First Day

The sun of the first day
    asked
at being's new emergence,
    Who are you?

    No answer.

Years passed.
    Day's last sun
asked a last question
    on the shore of the western sea
        in the silent evening,
           Who are you?

    No reply.

1941

Grief's Dark Night

Grief's dark night has visited my door
    again and again. I saw
the twisted grimace of pain, the macabre postures of fear
    its only weapon. A double-dealing in dark.

When I have heeded its mask of fear
    then – ruin and defeat.
    This sport of win-or-lose, life's false charade,
a miasma dogging all my steps from childhood,
    is loud with grief's mocking.

    This cinema of fear –
        Death's stage-craft has it flickering at night's core.

1941

The Path of Your Creation

The path of your creation you have kept festooned
    with the nets and traps of deception,
        Sorceress.

With cunning hand you have laid a snare of false trust
    for a simple soul.

No secret night did you set by for greatness,
    but branded it with this deceit.

The way your star illuminates for it,
    that is its inner way,
        forever shining clear.
With simple faith it is forever radiant.

Outwardly twisted it can be, but inwardly straight:
    this is its pride.

The wayfarer is mocked.
    Still he gains the truth
        in the depths of his being,
            bathed in light.

Nothing can deceive him.
    The final trophy
        he carries off to his store.

If he has been able to bear the deception lightly,
    he takes from your hand
        the imperishable right to peace.

1941

Glossary

Anga	A minor kingdom.
apsara	A dancing-girl of the heavens.
arati	A closing ceremony of worship.
Asharh	A month of the Bengali calendar: mid-June to mid-July (monsoon).
ashwattha	A large spreading fig-tree, the pipal, sacred to Hindus and to Buddhists.
Ashwin	Mid-September to mid-October.
Avanti	An old name for the region and city of Ujjain.
Baishakh	Mid-April to mid-May (the first month of the calendar).
bakul	An evergreen tree with white star-shaped flowers.
Baruni	Wife of Barun, god of rivers and oceans. The poet takes the name for a river in spate.
boukathako	A small bird that traditionally pleads with the shy bride to speak (literally "bride-speak-out").
Chaitra	Mid-March to mid-April (the last month of the calendar).
champa	An evergreen tree with orange-yellow flowers.
chokha-chokhi	Small river birds often seen in pairs.
crore	Ten million.
Dhaleshwari	A river in East Bengal, now Bangladesh.
Dhanapati	A merchant character in a sixteenth-century verse narrative.

Dhaumya	A priest.
Dipak-rag	A classical song associated with fire.
doël	A sweet-singing small bird.
Ganga	The Ganges river.
Gauri	A name for the goddess Durga, saviour and demon-slayer, and wife of Lord Shiva.
ghat	Steps leading down to a river; a boarding-place or landing place; a place of worship ceremonies.
Gorur	A mythical bird, vastly powerful, that carries Vishnu, the god of love.
Hastina	The capital of the Kaurava kingdom where princes compete in arts of weaponry.
jaam	A tree with dark plum-like fruit.
Janhu	A sage who was annoyed by the Ganga river and drank it up, later releasing it from his ear.
Jhilam	A river in the north of India (now Kashmir).
Joydev	A poet in Sanskrit of the twelfth century AD.
juthi	A white flower of the monsoon renowned for its scent.
Jyaishtha	Mid-May to mid-June.
kadam	A large tree bearing fragrant flowers in the rainy season.
kadamba	Another name for *kadam*.
kajol	Eye cosmetic.
Kankhal	A holy place where the river Ganga descends to the plain.
ketaki	A shrub with narrow leaves and white fragrant flowers.
keya	Another name for *ketaki*.
khanjana	A small bird distinguished by a frequent wagging of the tail.
kokil	A species of cuckoo.
Kripa	A guru.
kumkum	A red powder.

kunda	A climbing shrub with white flowers.
kurubak	This may be a red-flowering amaranth.
Kurukshetra	The battle-ground for the two warring sides, the Pandavas and the Kauravas, in the great epic *Mahabharata*.
lakh	A hundred thousand.
Lakshmi	The goddess of fortune. She is associated with prosperity, goodness and happiness.
lodhra	A pollen used by women as face-powder.
madhabi	A creeper of white flowers tinged with yellow.
malati	A climbing shrub with fragrant white flowers.
mallika	A variety of jasmine.
mugdal	The yellow lentil.
neepo	A tree with white-yellow circular flowers in the monsoon.
Om	The All. The holiest of sounds, containing in itself all sounds including silence, whose intonation is said to unite with the intonation pervading the universe.
paan	An evergreen creeper whose leaves are chewed with the areca nut.
parul	A summer-blooming tree with red trumpet-shaped flowers.
Phalgun	Mid-February to mid-March.
puja	An act of worship, individual or group. Also the festival of celebration of the goddess Durga.
Reba	A river in the Ujjain region.
Rudra	A name for Shiva, "The Terrible One".
rudra-veena	Smaller than the *veena* and of deeper tone. Its name suggests the awesome aspect of Shiva.
Shakuntala	The heroine of a famous Sanskrit play by Kalidas.
Shiva	The god of time, of destruction that must be, and lord of the dance. He bore down the great river Ganga from the heavens to Earth through his hair.

Sindhu-Baroyan	A light classical melody played or sung at day's end.
sindoor	A vermilion powder used by married women to mark the front crown of the head.
sitar	A traditional stringed instrument of lighter tone than the *veena*.
siuli	A tree that blossoms in autumn with small white flowers with an orange stem.
Srabon	Mid-July to mid-August (monsoon).
tamal	An evergreen tree with straight trunk and dark bark.
tambura	A four-stringed classical instrument.
Valmiki	The author of the *Ramayana* epic.
Vasuki	A name for the thousand-headed serpent that carries the world.
Veda-songs,	The *Vedas* are the primary scriptures of Hinduism. In large part they are hymns of praise.
veena	A traditional stringed instrument.
Vedic songs Vindhya	A mountain-range dividing the north of India from the south.

Notes

Cloud-Envoy (page 28)
This is a tribute to *Meghadutam* (*Meghdut*), the great Sanskrit poem by Kalidas, who lived (probably in the fifth century AD) in Ujjain, a sacred city in central India. Kalidas's poem is narrated by a Yaksha (a member of a class of demi-gods) who has been punished by his king with a year-long banishment from Alakā, the capital of the Yaksha realm. He pines for his wife in Alakā and requests a cloud to take her a message of love. As he describes the route to the cloud, a vivid and beautiful description of rain-swept India emerges.

To Ahalya (page 34)
Ahalya was married to a sage and the god Indra, desiring her, adopted the form of her husband to take advantage of her. The sage discovering them turned Ahalya to stone, in which form she continued in a suspended animation for many aeons until finally released and restored to life by the man-god Ram.

Swinging (page 46)
Jhulan or "swinging", the poem's title, is a day of festival to celebrate the courtship (as on a swing) of Radha and Krishna.

Song of the City (page 52)
a dream . . . a deer, dancing in dazzling gold In the *Ramayana* epic

Sita sees a golden deer and asks her husband Ram to catch it for her. While Ram runs after it the demon Ravana abducts Sita; the deer is an illusion he has arranged.

Brahmins are the senior caste, the priests and the teachers; *Kshatriyas* the warriors and rulers; *Vaishyas* the merchants and tradesmen; *Shudras* the menial labourers.

let the free horse run   A reference to an ancient ploy to lay claim to new territory.

Chitra (page 57)
The title carries the suggestion of a colourful enchantress and is a woman's name.

Urvashi (page 59)
A dancing-girl of the heavens, an *apsara*; the epitome of beauty.

Life's Monarch (page 62)
The Bengali title *Jibandebata* can mean "life-god". The word was Tagore's own and the concept of deep importance to him. It resists definition, yet in part may be said to be a guiding presence in life, to be discovered in ever-new revelation.

1400 (page 67)
1993 in the Bengali cultural calendar. The poem was written near the end of "1302".

Mother Bengal (page 69)
At that time Bengal included the area that is now Bangladesh.

Dream (page 74)
The writer takes the city of Kalidas as his setting. (See "Cloud-Envoy" above.)

my Malwa girl   The Ujjain region had the name Malwa.

Year's End (page 77)
Written on the last day of the Bengali year 1305.

Love-Tryst (page 82)
Tagore took the tale from a collection of Buddhist stories.

Karna and Kunti: A Dialogue (page 85)
With a light touch the poet deepens and expands an episode in the *Mahabharata* epic. Karna was Kunti's son by Surya, the Sun-God, and fostered by a lowly charioteer and his wife, Abhirath and Radha. He became a Kaurava general. Kunti later bore the three great kings Yudhisthira, Bhim and Arjuna, who command the Pandavas against the Kauravas in a war that seems to tell of all wars. Duryodhan is the mighty king who commands the Kauravas and has befriended Karna.

Krishna-Kali (page 101)
A dark-hued flower (literally "dark-bud"). A girl's name.

The Guest (page 103)
Written after the poet's wife, Mrinalini Devi, died in 1902.

Alone (page 104)
See "The Guest" above.

Death's Tryst (page 109)
The poet takes the marriage of Shiva as the epitome of thunderous celebration.

Song Offerings (page 118)
These are from *Gitanjali*, a book of 157 poems. Tagore used the Oriental title for a collection of 103 self-translations into English poetic prose, in the main from the eponymous volume but from nine others as well. The English *Gitanjali* won the Nobel Prize

in 1913 (see Introduction, p. 13). It has its own loveliness; but the original sequence is lighter, deeper, more telling. To about two-thirds of the original poems Tagore gave melodies and it is as songs that they are better known. But the spoken song has its own music.

Asharh (page 152)
The setting is the Ujjain countryside; Kalidas is indicated. See notes for "Cloud-Envoy" and "Dream" above.

The Game (page 153)
the deer of dreams See note for "Song of the City".

Hope (page 156)
I have omitted the poem's first part, that is merely introductory, and runs counter to the lyrical flow.

My Last Spring (page 158)
On a trip to South America in 1924 Tagore fell ill and convalesced in a villa outside Buenos Aires. His hostess was Victoria Ocampo (later a noted littérateur). The poem was for her.

Unafraid (page 162)
Cupid's darts The text has Pancham, who fires love-arrows of flowers. I have taken a translator's liberty.

Cornet (page 164)
Gopikanta Goshai's unctuous mind The name suggests a Vaishnavite, a worshipper of the god of love, Vishnu. His effusiveness (not a generic characteristic) is a far cry from the speaker's taciturnity.

Ordinary Girl (page 168)
Sarat-babu A term at once familiar and respectful for Sarat-chandra Chatterjee, a much-loved short-story writer and novelist

contemporary with the poet.

Alluding to *Urvashi* Tagore may have his own poem in mind, by now well-known.

a "seven-woman-warrior" attack Alludes to the death-struggle of Abhimanyu in the *Mahabharata* who is trapped in a ring of seven (male) warriors.

On the Bank of the Rup-Narayan (page 189)
The Rup-Narayan is the name of a river in Bengal and also means the world as the visible manifestation of God.

The Sun of the First Day (page 190)
Unable to write the poet dictated this and the final two poems from his death-bed.

Some Further Reading

Presentations of Tagore's verse in English include, beside the poet's own (see pages 13–14, 201–2):

I Won't Let You Go: Selected Poems translated by Ketaki Kushari Dyson, Bloodaxe Books, 1991
Selected Poems translated by William Radice, Penguin, 1985, 2005
Song Offerings translated by Joe Winter, Anvil Press Poetry, 2000

His fiction includes:

Gora translated by Sujit Mukherjee, Sahitya Akademi, 1998
The Home and the World translated by Surendranath Tagore, Macmillan, 1919
Selected Short Stories translated by William Radice, Penguin, 1991
Lipika (prose poems and short stories) translated by Joe Winter, Macmillan India, 2002

Plays include:

The Post Office translated by William Radice, The Tagore Centre UK, 1996

A biography that carries a good deal of information while touching the inner life less closely than Krishna Kripalani's *Rabindranath Tagore: a Biography* (OUP, London and the Grove Press, New York, 1962; see page 12) is *Rabindranath Tagore: the Myriad-Minded Man* by Krishna Dutta and Andrew Robinson, Bloomsbury, 1995.

A collection of autobiographical writings on the poetic journey is *Of Myself*, translated by Devadatta Joardar and Joe Winter, Anvil Press Poetry, 2006.

Index of Titles

BENGALI WRITING FROM ANVIL
Translated by Joe Winter

JIBANANANDA DAS
Bengal the Beautiful

The first English translation of 62 sonnets discovered in an exercise-book on Das's death in 1954, some twenty years after they were written. Infused with a scent of unrequited love, they were instantly popular when published and became a symbol of freedom in Bangladesh's War of Independence. Das captured the land's soul in these evocations of village life and natural beauty.

Naked Lonely Hand
SELECTED POEMS

A contemporary of Jibanananda Das (1899–1954) once described him as the 'loneliest poet'. In the preface to a selection he made of his own poetry he resisted the label, along with other attempts to classify him or his work. Joe Winter prefers to describe Jibanananda as 'a poet of perception. Whatever looks out that is most on its own within, in him is eloquent.'

RABINDRANATH TAGORE
Of Myself
TRANSLATED WITH DEVADATTA JOARDAR

The first English publication of a key collection of Tagore's autobiographical writings: six prose pieces, essays and lectures composed at landmark moments during the second half of his life. The collection focuses not only on poetry but on his many other interests, including religion and his world view. The essays provide an invaluable insight into the intellectual and spiritual world of a twentieth-century genius.

Song Offerings

Tagore won the Nobel Prize in 1913 primarily for this work, which he had rendered into English in the lucid grave prose of prayer. But his version, which also draws on other books, translates only about a third of *Gitanjali*'s lyrics. Joe Winter's complete translation, the first in English verse, emulates the grandeur and lightness of movement of these wonderful song-poems.